HOW GREAT THOU ART

HOW GREAT THOU ART

Poems of Nature and the Spirit

Including Four Sermons and a Story

David L. Coulter, M.D.

ISBN: 1979276633
ISBN 13: 9781979276634

Acknowlegement

The poems "June Solstice" and "River Ballad" were first published in the <u>American Journal of Geriatric Psychiatry</u> and are reprinted here with permission.

Nature Song

O for the sounds of a songbird's call
Drifting on the sky,

For a pillow of grass beneath my head
And the love-feast in my eye!

Come, my friend, share my bedroom,
My symphony without walls:

Whomsoever on earth will treasure this,
I will gladly give him all.

Table of Contents

Introduction

I wrote my first poem, "When the Wind Comes," when I was 12 years old. The poetic themes of nature and the spirit were evident even at that very young age. These themes have continued to inspire me throughout my life. This collection bring together all of the poems I have written during my life that reflect these interrelated themes. Some of the poems are as immature as I was at the time I wrote them, while others reflect a lifetime of experiences and years spent in contemplation of nature and spirituality. The emotional tone of the poems ranges from awe and joy to fear and depression, from doubt and uncertainty to trust and faith, from peace and quiet to raging anxiety, and from philosophical searching to theological inquiry. The collection of poems presented here is as complex as life itself, with more hard questions than easy answers. The constantly changing presence of nature and spirituality in these poems still somehow provides a unifying vision, from which I hope the reader might extract some useful insight. Poets write hundreds of poems but are fortunate if even a couple of them are remembered. I have no illusions in that regard but hope that at least a few of the poems in this collection might resonate with the reader.

The title of this collection is based on the hymn of the same name:

"O Lord my God, when I in awesome wonder
Consider all the worlds thy hands have made,
I see the stars, I hear the rolling thunder,

Thy power throughout the universe displayed,
Then sings my soul, my savior God, to thee,
How great thou art! How great thou art!"

The **first part**, "The Almanack of Faith," was written when my wife was having serious health problems and I needed a way to cope with that. I did not have a plan when I started the project, but rather waited until each month began and then looked for an inspiration that was related to that particular time of year. It is thus a true almanac of ideas and images drawn from the continuous cycles of time and nature.

The **second part**, "Syllogisms of Faith," is in some ways an homage to Thomas Aquinas and a kind of "Summa Theologica" written from the perspective of nature and spirituality. The first syllogism presents a "proof of God" in a format Aquinas might have appreciated. It is in fact an explication of my own transformative experience of faith, when in one brief moment a lifetime of searching for faith all came together for me. The Thomistic and Aristotelian themes continue in the second and third syllogisms. Every line in these poems is based on a theological or philosophical idea. My goal in writing this was to present a coherent and philosophically sound justification of faith based on nature and God's presence in the world. Perhaps Professor Aquinas might give me a B+ for my effort.

The **third part** presents the poems I have written throughout my adult life related to nature and spirituality. Many are explained by the attached notes. Some I should probably be ashamed to share with the reader, but they are included here to provide balance. Most were written because I had to and then put away in my notebooks and never shared with anyone until now.

The **fourth part** is included to encourage young readers to follow their muse and write whenever nature or the spirit moves them. Youthful scribblings like these can be the prelude to a lifetime of poetry. Too many young people write poems in their youth but then turn away when the demands of life and career draw them to other pursuits. I confess to this too, since my poetic efforts declined as I was pursuing my academic career.

But my muse was only dormant, not lost, and was finally reawakened later in my life. The title of this part is also a sly reference to Wordsworth's great poem, "Intimations of Immortality from Recollections of Early Childhood."

The **fifth part** consists of four sermons and a story. I have been privileged to be able to give a few sermons at my church on a variety of topics. As a layman I appreciate the trust my pastor had in allowing me to take the pulpit to present these ideas. The story, which was written when I was a teenager, is included to encourage all young people to fight the racism that was present in my own youth and is still present today. A radical belief in equality, a love for everyone regardless of skin color or anything else, a commitment to peace and justice, a humble faith in God, and the courage to stand up for what one believes, will always provide the guidance one needs in order to deal with the demands of today and tomorrow.

Part One
The Almanack of Faith

JANUARY BEGINS

The snow blows past the bleak and barren stone
While January's ice encumbers thoughts
That hibernate in slumber, now alone,
False comforts lost when clarity was sought.

This new year's quiet landscape yields no peace
To earnest pilgrims, yearning souls enrolled
In one great quest that cannot ever cease
But may, some day, relieve this dolorous cold.

Having left behind what went before
And knowing nothing of what lies ahead,
Still skeptic, we proceed, and trust that more
Experience will lead to faith instead.

So whether we be young, mature or old,
To honest conscience we must tightly hold.

NOTES:

- This poem is a revision of a poem I wrote when I was 19 years old (dated April, 1967). The challenge in revising it was to see if the ideas were still relevant almost 50 years later. The teenage version was written when I was trying to get rid of everything other people had told me to believe and I was searching for what it was that I really believed for myself. This is the 1967 original:

Snow on stone will numb the eye
And stony snow encumber thought,
While conscious pride so dearly bought
Now stifles comfort in a silent sigh.

There is a love---there is a peace
That overcomes the dolorous cold
I see in things, my soul enrolled
In a fruitless search that will not cease.

The quest of happiness is my goal,
But nothing found relieves the pain.
And so in honesty, I must retain
The conscience of a skeptic soul.

- January is named after the Roman god Janus, who is usually represented with two faces, one looking backward and one looking forward. The poem reflects that spirit, especially in the third stanza.
- The first part of the poem reflects the Christian hymn, "In the Bleak Midwinter," written by Christina Rossetti:

In the bleak mid-winter
Frosty wind made moan,
Earth stood hard as iron,
Water like a stone;
Snow had fallen, snow on snow,
Snow on snow,
In the bleak mid-winter
Long ago.

Our God, Heaven cannot hold Him
Nor earth sustain;
Heaven and earth shall flee away
When He comes to reign:

In the bleak mid-winter
A stable-place sufficed
The Lord God Almighty,
Jesus Christ.

Enough for Him, whom cherubim
Worship night and day,
A breastful of milk,
And a mangerful of hay;
Enough for Him, whom angels
Fall down before,
The ox and ass and camel
Which adore.

Angels and archangels
May have gathered there,
Cherubim and seraphim
Thronged the air -
But only His mother
In her maiden bliss
Worshipped the Beloved
With a kiss.

What can I give Him,
Poor as I am?
If I were a shepherd
I would bring a lamb;
If I were a wise man
I would do my part;
Yet what I can, I give Him -
I give my heart.

- Lines 11-12 reflects the classic Quaker proverb, "Proceed as the way opens."

FEBRUARY

The frigid wind disturbs the weathered stones
Half covered by accumulated snow,
Where winter's quilt now warms the sleeping bones
Of those I loved alive so long ago,

Their precious names obscured, but still engraved
Upon my soul, as I stand reflecting here
In winter's gloom, the storm that I have braved
Surrounding me with sounds of mortal fear.

And yet this shortest month, so dark and cold,
Recalls again and celebrates the birth
Not only of the dead whose love I hold,
But also those I love, still living on this earth:

I will not stay here long, instead embrace
The legacies of loss redeemed in grace.

MARCH EQUINOX

From whence arrives the life that swells the seed
And stirs the fledgling bird inside its shell?
From whence derives the soul, so newly keyed
To womb-bound babies' beating hearts as well?

New birth impends, not yet quite here, gestating,
As cycling earthly seasons of the year
Are joined to timeless human spirit, waiting
For the light of nascent springtime to appear.

The dying winter ends as something new,
Emerging in commingled life and soul,
Is surging forth with joy to soon imbue
The world with twice-born life, renewed and whole.

As robins sing and flowers bloom, so we await
And celebrate what earth and grace create.

See also John 3:5, "Unless a person is born through water and
the spirit, he cannot enter the kingdom of God."

ANOTHER APRIL

The greening leaves of dormant grass arrive,
By longer days awakened, to suggest
A newly warming April comes alive
Fur us, for whom another year has blessed.

Recalling Aprils past, whose joys we knew,
Now grateful to be here again, today,
With open arms we welcome Nature's preview
Of the glories that will soon arrive in May.

Will April come again for us next year?
We cannot know, but hope and pray it will;
As overtures of spring ring bright and clear,
We focus faith on joys today will fill:

To humbly walk with God * our only reason,
We celebrate another April season.

*see Micah 6:8

MAY IS BUD SEASON (1)

These barren branches, bleak and leafless, bud
On Concord vines beside my kitchen porch,
There quickened by labruscan blood (2), a flood
Of blossoms opened by May's sun-bright torch,

As I sit in peace here, contemplating
The joys of fearless life 'neath fig and vine,
A Kingdom promised once to all (3), awaiting
The fruits of justice, mercy (4), love and wine.

I have done my best to live as I was told,
Renounced the sword when I became a man (5),
And banished fear, secured by faith I hold
In worlds I cannot see, and buds I can:

So lead me gently home (6) your way, to play
Where leafing vines bring shelter here today.

1. All New Englanders know that "March is mud season," so the title of this poem is a pun on that knowledge.
2. The scientific name for a Concord grapevine is "Vitis labrusca."
3. See Micah 4: 3-4: "He will judge between many peoples and will settle disputes for strong nations far and wide. They shall beat their swords into plowshares and their spears into pruning hooks. Nation will not take up the sword against another nation, nor will they study war any more. Every man will sit under his vine and fig

tree, and no one will make him afraid, for the Lord almighty has spoken."

4. See Micah 6: 8, "He has shown you, O mortal, what is good. And what does the Lord require of you? To act justly and to love mercy and to walk humbly with your God."

5. I declared that I was a Christian pacifist when I was 21 years old, and have been faithful to that commitment ever since.

6. See the wonderful old Christian hymn:

Lead me gently home, Father,
Lead me gently home,
When life's toils are ended
And parting days have come;
Sin no more shall tempt me,
Ne'er from thee I'll roam;
If Thou will only lead me, Father,
Lead me gently home.

JUNE SOLSTICE

Springtime's rippling hormones peak in June,
Rambunctious nature's energized creation
Rising taut, flamboyant, gone too soon
To seed, the fruit of this year's generation.

Is there a solstice in our time here on earth,
An age of cresting vigor, strength and power,
When perfumed hormones pulsing from our birth
Fill resplendent days with bounteous flower?

Or are there many days of longest light
And many zeniths all throughout our years,
The solstices of love and wise insight
And perigees of faith when grace appears?

The pleasures of this summer day remain
For us to have today and have again.

WITH PLATO IN JULY

Lying near the lilies, on the grass
Beneath the mid-day sun, the July sky
Alive and hot, as years through ages pass,
Maturing gifts of wisdom (1) in my eyes,

I think of my vocation, vows I made (2)
When callow youth upon my body reigned,
A ministry in debt (as yet unpaid)
For youthful love of beauty I've retained.

This July day I ask, what have I done,
And wonder still, in wonders I still see:
Have I been true to promises begun
Now forty years from when I came to be?

I see my answer here this summer day
In debts I am still eager to repay.

1. See Plato's <u>Symposium,</u> in which Socrates recalls Diotima's view of
   love (the following analysis is from the SparkNotes website):

   Diotima describes love as the pursuit of beauty in a grad-
   ual ascent from the particular to the general, culminating
   in an understanding of the Form of Beauty. Even the most

ignorant soul is drawn to beauty on some level. What most of us don't realize, she suggests, is that what attracts us to a beautiful person, for instance, is that we perceive in that person an idea of the greater Form of Beauty. That is, we are attracted not to the person but to the beauty in the person. If our love is keen enough, we will not be satisfied by beautiful people but will seek out beauty in more generalized forms: in minds, in the structure of a well-ordered state, and ultimately in the Form of Beauty itself, the most generalized form that beauty takes.

2. When I turned thirty, I wrote:

    Never again in innocence
    Will we be happy as a child---
    But we still see, and will always be
    In loving beauty young and free;
    While there is breath and blood and strength,
    What we were will guide us yet,
    For we have lost the eyes of childhood,
    Seeing now with childlike manhood.

FOREVER AUGUST

The garden grows unweeded and unruly
As newly ripe tomatoes, plump and red,
Join blooming Sharon roses, blessing truly
These magic August days that spread ahead.

Approaching time for harvest, coming soon,
The evening stars in Leo shining bright,
Creation's chorus sings a joyous tune
As life slows down, yet still is fresh tonight.

Beneath an August sky my life began,
A mewling babe with new immortal soul,
And under August sunshine, woman and man,
We vowed immortal love our married goal.

Some day the time of harvest will arrive,
But what is now eternal will survive.

(vaguely with reference to Matthew 13: 24-30)

SEPTEMBER EQUINOX

Picking ripened grapes from off the vine,
Extracting and fermenting their sweet juice,
The transformation starts to make the wine,
Which is their purpose and their fruitful use.

The days still warm, the nights becoming cool,
As summer yields its bounty to the fall,
September gives a promise of renewal
When equinox next cycles nature's call.

Today the wine, like life, will start to age
With hopes it will improve in years to come;
Its vintage young, we trust its final stage
Fulfills the loving nurture it came from.

A lifetime is required, all things agreeing,
In order to create a human being.*

*See John S. Dunne, "Dark Light of Love," 2014, page 48

COHOLETH IN OCTOBER

For every thing that ends is a beginning,
For every winter, there will come a spring,
For every sacrament, a time for sinning,
For every quiet time, a time to sing.

October's dying leaves enrich the ground
While earth revokes the promises it made,
But greater riches still may yet be found
In vanities redeemed while seasons fade.

Life cycles, we do not, we live and die
And long for happiness in all we do;
Anticipating joy, we bravely try
To let the old truths show us what is new.

These vanities will vanish with belief
That banishes what gives us no relief.

This poem is primarily a meditation on Ecclesiastes, chapter 3, but it is also informed by John 10:10, "I have come so that you may have life more abundantly."

NOVEMBER SNOWFALL

November skies provide the virgin snow
That gently welcomes the approaching season,
Not yet too soon, but not too late to know
That hard times sometimes come for no known reason.

November is a time for preparation,
The pantry full, the furnace running well,
All things arrayed in sharp anticipation
Of challenges the world cannot foretell.

This year will end next month and be reborn
With faithful guarantees of life next year,
Reminding us to trust and not to mourn
Our loss, because we know, these skies will clear.

What more can we do now than just hold steady
And pray that what comes next will find us ready?

1.   See Mark 13:32-37:

"But about that day or hour no one knows, not even the
angels in heaven, nor the Son, but only the Father. Be on
guard! Be alert[a]! You do not know when that time will
come. It's like a man going away: He leaves his house and
puts his servants in charge, each with their assigned task,
and tells the one at the door to keep watch. Therefore

keep watch because you do not know when the owner of the house will come back—whether in the evening, or at midnight, or when the rooster crows, or at dawn. If he comes suddenly, do not let him find you sleeping. What I say to you, I say to everyone: 'Watch!'"

2. See also the classic hymn "Unclouded Day" by J.K. Alwood (1880)

O they tell me of a home far beyond the skies,
O they tell me of a home far away;
O they tell me of a home where no storm clouds rise,
O they tell me of an unclouded day.

WINTER SOLSTICE

With twilight starting in the afternoon,
The longest, darkest night on earth begins,
The world now curled beneath December's moon
While memory of summer's pleasure dims,

The planet now most distant from the sun,
But never far from God's eternal Light
Enduring still, as promised, night undone
By candles of His love, forever bright.

With covenants of peace and joys to come
When darkness yields and next the dawn arrives,
Our faith abides, emerging, fragile, numb,
But confident in knowing hope survives.

For earth still turns this winter solstice eve
And this great Light confirms what we believe.

REFERENCES

1. John 1: 4-5, "All that came to be had life in him, and that life was
    the Light of men, a Light that shines in the darkness, a Light that
    darkness cannot overpower."
2. John 8: 12, "I am the Light of the world, anyone who follows me
    will not be walking in the dark, but will have the light of life."

3. Luke 2:8-10, "The angel of the Lord appeared to them and the glory of the Lord shone around them. The angel said, do not be afraid, I bring you news of great joy, a joy to be shared with all people."

4. "The story of Chanukkah is preserved in the books of the First and Second Maccabees. The miracle of the one-day supply of oil miraculously lasting eight days is first described in the Talmud. The Gemara (Talmud), in tractate Shabbat, page 21b, focuses on Shabbat candles and moves to Chanukkah candles and says that after the forces of Antiochus IV had been driven from the Temple, the Maccabees discovered that almost all of the ritual olive oil had been profaned. They found only a single container that was still sealed by the High Priest, with enough oil to keep the menorah in the Temple lit for a single day. They used this, yet it burned for eight days." (text recovered from the web)

Part Two
Syllogisms of Faith

.

FIRST SYLLOGISM OF FAITH

The osprey soars on wide-stretched wings
Above her fledgling's treetop nest,
Whose hungry cries are heard below
On forest paths, where insects crawl
Among the hidden flowers there---
All creation, great and small,
Alive with glory graced from God---
                For God is love

The love is in the land and sky
And all that God has made on earth,
In beasts and birds, and people, too,
A light that shines upon the world
Illuminating every heart,
Unrestrained and bursting through
The darkest prisons of the soul---
                For love just is

So what of all with life and breath
Can overcome our destiny
To die, as all creation must?
Not fortune, fame, or glory, power,
But love alone can outlive death,
The love that God gives us to use,
Which we can not increase or lose---
                For God just is

SECOND SYLLOGISM OF FAITH

The sounds of nature resonate
When we become aware of them,
But in the silence that surrounds us,
When we are centered in the stillness
That precedes the sounds we hear,
Just then we hear a different voice,
Before, beyond, bespoke, beloved---
    So listen for God's voice

As fragrant blooms of spring proclaim
The pain of winter is forgiven,
So too the God of all creation lives,
Forgives us with divine assent
To all the world's unruliness,
A voice we do not hear but feel,
Now speaking to out shriven hearts---
    God speaks through love

As leaves of past years fall and die
But nourish roots of next year's spring,
So we are nourished by the love
Of all who lived in joy before us,
And so we listen, silent, for the love
That opens up our hearts and souls,
Accepting all that was, will be---
    We listen to the love

THIRD SYLLOGISM OF FAITH

So, what is truth? All Nature knows
Abundant life that multiplies
And celebrates the world's creation,
In birds and beasts and lilies of the field,
A truth from God we find in love
And not in mere philosophy,
To which we can entrust our lives---
    For love is trust

When darkness comes, I am afraid
To be alone in woods or water,
Except when I release my soul
To God, who keeps me safe today
With promises of joy to come,
As winter's barren cold gives way
To resurrected life in spring---
    For trust is faith

My soul is swollen, filled with love
For all that is, has been, will be,
The living and eternal Spirit
Of the silence and the joy,
A joy that grows when I believe
In God who came into our world
To reconcile all of creation---
    For faith is joy

Part Three
Nature, Faith and Spirituality

My Place
A Song for the Saint Lawrence River

My place is here upon this ridge
Of glaciated granite stone
Among the lichens, moss and trees
And pleasant rocks I call my own.

My place is here bathed by the river,
Immersed, suspended, swimming free
Astride the gentle currents flowing
Past these islands to the sea.

My place is here within these woods
Of ash and maple, oak and pine,
All senses keened to all that thrives
Where nature, time and life align.

My place is anywhere I am
Surrounded by the world's creation,
In which I only wish to live
With humble thanks and adoration.

Trinity
A Hymn of Faith

O **Father**, please look for me sitting down here
At the back of the church in an empty, dark pew,
Aware of my failings, contrite and sincere,
A <u>sinner</u> desiring forgiveness from you.

I know that the **Son of God** will always be with me
However I need him, wherever I go,
But my faith still may waver while I'm struggling to be
A <u>seeker</u> of grace only He can bestow.

So come, **Holy Spirit**, and show me the way
To use what I have to help those who have needs,
Because I am trying to live every day
As a <u>servant</u> pursuing your Will through my deeds.

The first stanza recalls Luke 18:11-14. The second stanza recalls the haiku I wrote ("Wherever I am//In any way I need him//Jesus always comes.") The fourth line of this stanza also recalls the life journey of John Newton who wrote "Amazing Grace." Indeed, this hymn can be sung to the same tune as "Amazing Grace." The last line of course refers to the Lord's Prayer, "Thy Will be done on earth as it is in Heaven." It is up us to make that happen.

Moses Was an African

Chaim goes to temple
With his friend Tahounia.
He is from Jerusalem,
She is from Ethiopia.
They worship together---
    Because Moses was an African.

Jamirah goes to the mosque
With her friend Abdullah.
She is from Aleppo,
He is from Nigeria.
They worship together---
    Because Moses was an African.

Cristiane goes to Mass
With her friend Tebogo.
She is from Sicily,
He is from South Africa.
They worship together---
    Because Moses was an African.

- Moses was born in Goshen, which is part of Egypt, and thus part of Africa (see Exodus 2: 1-9).
- Chaim means "life," Tahounia means "staying with us."
- Jamirah means "handsome," Abdullah means "servant of God."
- Cristiane refers to Christ, Tebogo means "thankful."

Blow Out the Candle

An Easter Vigil

I climbed a tree to hear the sounds
Of wind and water late tonight,
Tracing moonlit constellations
Through endless space into my heart.
The dark dominion now in power
Holds in hand all living things
Loving blackness, in communion
With the ruler of the night.

For day to be, the night must live,
For Light to be, the night must give
Like praise and glory to creation,
Night and morning made as one
On that first day, the Earth begun.
I love the creatures that emerge
When daylight ends and darkness rules,
As much as all that live in light.

I climbed but could not reach the stars,
Who sent me down to stand once more
With birds and beasts amidst the swamp.
Yet now I think of Him who went
To darkness where there is no light,
To reconcile in love the souls
In evil bound, forlorn, condemned,
Who languish in eternal night.

Noisy lanterns drove me hence,
Fearful lanterns lit in loathing
Of my lonesome rendezvous.
Leave the night-dispersing light---
Daylight has its time and place.
Bless the darkness, bless the night,
For what is dark will yet be bright,
And bless the love that makes it right.

NOTE: This is a theologically complicated poem. The first image is the "dark night of the soul," and then there is a reference to Genesis in the second stanza, (as well as to John's Gospel 8:12, "I am the Light of the world, whoever follows me will never walk in darkness, but will have the light of life.). Then there is a reference to the Easter story in the third stanza (Jesus descending into Hell between the crucifixion and the resurrection). And the last stanza tries to tie it all together (as in Psalm 139, 1-12: If I say, "Surely the darkness will hide me and the light become night around me," even the darkness will not be dark to you; the night will shine like the day, for darkness is as light to you).

Oasis

'Twas just a simple medal on a chain,
A small religious thing my parents gave
For me to wear, a talisman so plain
I did not know they prayed that it would save

My soul and keep me safe from all despair,
And so when fearsome winds of faithless doubt
Arrived, I lost what they had hoped to share
And thought that childish medal was thrown out.

I wandered in the desert for a while
And had no sense of purpose or a guide
To find what I had lost through my denial
Of all that little medal signified.

But I kept looking, longing for the way
To reach the green oasis, just ahead,
Whose pool I hoped would cleanse and wash away
The trackless sand and nourish me instead.

Years passed before I found my heart's desire
And drank sweet water from that desert spring,
And felt that unlost medal draw me nigher
To long-sought peace and joyful flourishing.

But surrounding the oasis I could see
The shifting, windswept, burning dunes of doubt,
And a shimmering mirage attracting me
With illusions I might never be without.

You cannot find a thing you have not lost
And so, sometimes, you have to let it go,
But always know the search is worth the cost,
An oasis guaranteed to make it so,

Because an oasis requires the desert sand,
And to be refreshing, water must have thirst,
A saving medal needs troubles to withstand,
And desert denied will only make life worse.

NOTES:

1. "Doubt is not the opposite of faith; it is one element of faith"
   (Paul Tillich)
2. Faith without doubt is zealotry (or terrorism)
3. The medal represents faith, the oasis represents acceptance.
4. I acknowledge my debt to the Bible books of Job and Ecclesiastes.
5. See also Matthew 4: 1-11.

On a Day Like Today
August 12, 2013

On a day like today

The Swami sat in silence here
To think of healing, the rain not feeling,
In meditation by the river,
Young, at peace, not long to live
But living at this place forever.

Another day not like today

Underneath a river of ice
So many thousand years ago,
And long before this river flowed,
Pebbles scraping ancient rock
Carved the stripes I see today.

On other days just like today

My friends were born, and lived, and died
But never came to share this space,
This quiet place of peace and joy,
Nor sat with me, nor ever will
Except their souls be with me still.

On many days just like today

As seasons pass and years go by,
The river flows and insects fly,
While birds sing out and deer run free,
Around this place, unseen to me
Once present, now so far away.

But on this day of life today

My arms outstretched embrace the sky,
The woods and rocks, as all around
The world surrounds me where I stand
Or sit where Swami's peace abounds,
The universal prayer we share.

How blessed I am this day today

To be alive to celebrate
The gift of life this bounteous day
(A gift denied to friends who have died),
My gift to them the chance to play
And live again through me today.

On every day, not just today

I will be faithful, will not stray,
For some may walk these woods, not seeing,
But I will strive to see, not walking,
And simply pray, in my own way,
Like blessed Francis, all my days.

I offered in church "A prayer of thanksgiving for the gift of being alive on a day like today," which immediately made me realize that this should be the title of the poem, and also led me to add the sixth stanza.

Elegy Written in an Ohio Churchyard

Go into the woods and climb the rocks
To find the pristine little pool
That lies in peaceful solitude
And stillness there, where all around
Is verdant and abundant life.

The pool is deep and bottomless,
Or so it seems when standing by
The water's edge, the endless sky
Reflected there, a reservoir
With no beginning and no end.

Now close your eyes and ease your self
Into the pool and feel the water,
Immerse your body and your mind
In cleansing water, wondering
From whence this peaceful stillness comes.

Can you perceive the pool's two springs
That flow together in this pond?
One source is warm and feels like tears
Of sadness, seeking solace there
Until it merges with the other,

A swirling, sweet, refreshing stream
That rises up from deep within
To wash away the tearful fear,
A gentle current, cool and calming,
Two waters joined in harmony.

O I could stay and swim again
And live my life within this pool,
Whose springs, like two united souls,
Can not be separated here today
Or in the days that are to come.

The poem was written in memory of my college friend Dean Ryan, who was Jonathan to my David (see 1 Sam 18:1, "The soul of Jonathan was merged with the soul of David and they became as one soul.") The poem also recalls Thomas Gray's "Elegy Written in a Country Churchyard," which concludes with this Epitaph:

Here rests his head upon the lap of earth
A youth to fortune and to fame unknown.
Fair science frowned not on his humble birth,
And melancholy marked him for her own.

Large was his bounty, and his soul sincere,
Heaven did a recompense as largely send:
He gave to misery all he had, a tear,
He gained from Heaven ('twas all he wished) a friend.

No farther seek his merits to disclose,
Or draw his frailties from their dread abode,
(There they alike in trembling hope repose)
The bosom of his Father and his God.

Song to the Huron River

Cold,
Banks bundled in folded ice
That wraps the weaving river's shallows,
Freely runs the riving channel,
Bearing frozen, icy fragments
In portents of an early death:

    Time passes. The river endures.

Tame,
But mindful of an earlier time
That witnessed a wintry wilderness,
Gamely fights the freezing water,
Taking the dam's delivered flow
In its effort to be free:

    Time passes. The river endures.

Faith,
Sustained by simple courage
That bears with grace what it is given,
Gladly guides an honest world,
Knowing ice will surely end
In days of springtime soon to be:

    Time passes. The river endures.

River Ballad

I.
Torrential rain, a sudden summer squall,
Sends rivulets that soak the thirsty earth
And join in freshets towards a waterfall,
A nascent stream in new formed robust birth,

Each drop so rare and precious, multiplied
By every other drop that forms the course,
All surge together, impact magnified,
And swell the pond that is the river's source.

II.
The outlet of the rain-filled little pond
Grows larger as it drains the summer flood
And carries all the droplets far beyond
Their origin, free-flowing, like fresh blood

That vivifies the land and life downstream,
Becoming first a creek and then a river,
Its current amplified with youthful dreams
That challenge limits which its banks deliver.

III.
The river plunges, smashing past the rocks
And crashing on the rapids as it goes,

Then settles down, constrained by dams and locks
And folks content with how the river flows,

And yet, within the river, drops endure
That still recall the thunder of their birth,
But cannot slow the flow that time ensures
Will someday end the promise of their worth.

IV.
The river has matured, but still it carries,
In calm and fragrant currents that conceal
The snags and bars that threaten the unwary,
The risks no river forecast could reveal,

And still it bears the drops that bring new life
By irrigating fields along the plain,
Invigorating all with strength and rife
With fruitful growth that renews life again.

V.
But ah, the aging river, safely past
Those snares and dangers, all its duties done,
Meandering in peace throughout the vast
Inheritance its ancient valley won,

In loops and bends across the fertile land
Now passes oxbow graves of what it was,
Toward the place no river can withstand,
Where nature cycles all that water does.

VI.
The drops that traveled to the river's end,
Where delta swampland stretches far and wide,
Born long ago in many storms, now send
Whatever was, is now and will abide

To meet the waiting, welcome, timeless sea
That will envelop all the river gives,
But yet they trust that their identity
For all eternity will somehow live.

VII.
These drops that came from thunder to the sea
Are all unique and special, yet as one
They have become what they will always be
Long after their great river trip is done,

But our life journey, glorious and grand,
Has no need now to end, today or ever,
Our final port remaining yet unplanned,
With much to do between now and forever.

The First Supper

A Psalm From Another David

This is the day I celebrate.
At last, today I know what I am
And where tomorrow seems to be.

My Father crowds my memory
When I recall whose son I am
And contemplate return to him.

But Father, I am frightened now
To come home, close to you again
Where love is a new and fragile thing.

And so this fearful love is mediated,
Joyous in concelebration
With the friend by whom I am.

Seldom have I felt this sense
Of integrity, of happiness,
As in communion with him now.

Body and soul, I long for him
Near me now, near me always,
Near me on my journeys home.

With me today as I go out
To meet you, Father, and tomorrow,
His hand on mine will make me strong.

This is a complex poem with multiple layers of meaning. It is, of course, a metaphor of conversion and faith, hence the title, of trusting in Jesus to lead me home to God's love. On a literal level, it is also about coming home and being close to my own father again. And it is also a poem about friendship, trust and love, the power of which has never dimmed.

The Lord's Prayer Revised for Love

Our Father, who lives in Heaven, hallowed be your name.
May your kingdom come to us through your love for all people on earth,
And may your will be done when we love others as you love us,
Every day here on earth as it will be forever in Heaven.
Give us this day the strength we need to do your will,
And forgive us when we do not see your love in those we meet,
As we forgive those whose love is hidden from us.
Lead us not into the temptations of hate and violence against others,
But deliver us from the evil that is the absence of your love,
For yours is the love that is from God, of God and to God,
Forever and ever,
Amen.

The Bible says that "God is love" (1 John 4:8) and that the most important commandments are to "Love God with all of your heart, mind and soul," and "To love one another as you love yourself" (Matthew 22: 37-39). So why does the conventional version of the Lord's Prayer not mention love? This revision is an attempt to bridge this gap. After I wrote it I waited for the fire and brimstone to rain down upon my head for blasphemy, but when nothing happened, I figured God was okay with it.=

The Lord's Prayer Revised for Meaning

Our Father, who art in Heaven, hallowed be thy name.

Loving Creator, who lives in us and sustains us, we praise you and thank you for your all-encompassing care for us.

Thy Kingdom, come.

We pray now that the peaceable Kingdom, which consists of your eternal love for all of your creation, will come to us and guide us to do what you ask of us, joining us together in all of our diversity.

Thy will be done, on earth as it is in Heaven.

Send us the Holy Spirit to show us how to do your will today and every day. Not our will, but your will be done. Give us the strength to love others as you love them. Help us to work for universal peace, justice and equality in accordance with your will.

Give us this day our daily bread.

Grant to us today what you know we need to nourish us, body, mind and soul, so that we may follow the path that you have made for us. We understand that your bread, like the manna you sent to the Israelites in the desert, cannot be saved for another day, so we trust that you will always provide for us as we start every day.

Forgive us our debts, as we forgive our debtors.

We trust in your forgiveness for the times when we have been unkind or unfaithful to your Word. Help us to forgive ourselves, as we continue with your help to forgive those who have been unkind to us.

Lead us not into temptation, but deliver us from evil.

Do not let our faith in you be tested again in times of trial, through our weakness, but rather fill us with your love, which will keep us safe today, tomorrow and forever.

For thine is the Kingdom, the power and the glory.

For we believe in the love that is from God, of God and to God, forever and ever.

Amen.

~~

This is an attempt to expand on the well-known words of the prayer and to explain what they might mean to those of us who recite it every day.

The Lake

Not yet twilight. The lake:
Like liquid gold, as nature, creation:
Being without bottom, being without end.
Surface bearing me, carrying my image---
Does it, so doing, possess me as well?
This lake, this water, this well of the world,
Will I know it again as it was before,
Will the image on the silvery surface, serene,
Ever be to me as I am to myself?

Ocean of being, matrix of life,
Sheltering those whose lives demand it,
As within them flows, needed and unnoticed,
That through which they flow themselves---
The lake, lying limitless, source of all life.
Such unanimity, anonymity,
Can we know the union of creator and creation?
The lake is their life; what, whose is mine?
What flows in me to compare with them?

Noon. Blue sky above, blue lake below,
I in between.
The lake: heaven seen in its depth---
Are its roots too them in heaven?
When so, then where am I?
All nature uniting, with one exclusion,
Conspiring against me, I who am hers.

But yet, do not I (as the lake)
Bear heaven also, inside myself?

Leaves fall, loosed from the trees,
Dry and die on the ground, life lost.
Leaves in the lake, sustained, live on
But shortly, and regardless, die.
The lake, from which the leaves took life,
The source, now drowns them in its purity,
The essence of being, immersed in which
Non-human nature cannot survive.
Human, can I?
Regain, retain the source, alive?

What is the shore, but not-lake?
Permeating it contains, yet remains,
Resplendent, noticed because it is noticeable,
Tenuous, yet tenaciously clinging to this:
That it is not-lake. I too am of the land:
In me alone and lonely the matrix
Of whom I am and to whom I go.
Distinct, despairing, my dirge is then
That I am as I am and will be not.

The lake: tempter, brothel of man,
Man existent, prostituting existence.
For who would not (to gain the lake of peace)
Stand and wish, hope, demand for succor?
What avails it him to chase the idols of his self?

Tear away, abhor, ignore the water
(How sweet, certain, silken it ripples!)
Folly to think thereof: unless I be lake,
Far better to live than to hope.

The poem was written in the fall of 1966 when I was a 19 year old sophomore at the University of Notre Dame. It is about St. Mary's Lake, which is on the campus there. Whenever I was troubled and searching for spiritual guidance, a long walk around the lake always provided what I needed.

Who Walks With Me
(Response to <u>The Lake</u>)

Let's go to the lake once more, my friend,
And walk the long path all around
From bank to shore and home again,

And talk about the things that count,
Like love and death and truth and beauty,
The simple courage of an honest life.

Or maybe just walk side by side
In silence, listening to the sounds
Of waves and water, wind and leaves.

I thought I came here all alone
And never knew that you were there
Beside me, waiting faithfully

For me to see and feel your touch,
To hear your voice inside my soul,
Knowing that our time would come.

Now walk with me again together
Beyond this lake and everywhere
We go, apart no more forever.

Making Out at Bennett Place

Locked in arms of love
We made out at Bennett Place,
Where armies met in confrontation,
Met to talk, to make out a paper,
The end of war, the Civil War.

I can almost make out their faces, dirty, tired,
Emptied of the terrible ideals
With which they went to joyous war,
Now weary for an end to it, any end,
At first too generous and overruled,
But done at last, consummated.

I can embrace at Bennett Place,
I can feel simple human beings all around me
Arm in arm, enthusiastic again,
Returning home to family, farm and bed,
Smiling on two lovers making out.

I could never love at Gettysburg.
A bloated smell of death reigns forever
On that bloody battlefield:
I think of broken hearts, empty beds and unplowed fields.

But here, here in Durham, Carolina,
Enemies were made men, and men made lovers,
Here I lose myself in the arms of my beloved.

A Watcher of Days

Watcher of days and observer of skies
And air's changed color in dawn-light,
By work imprisoned inside windows,
Something rises to stick in me:
Perhaps it is the lust of poetry
That cannot now be consummated.
I think it is duty triumphant over love.

Bugling sounds of majesty,
Louder the bluer and charged the day,
Blast me free for reveille,
True soldier of the universe,
Watcher of any happenstance
All equally overwhelming.

When days so hold me, I speak out loud,
Not to share my lament of confinement
But as a guerrilla recruiting friends.

A Song of Change

The night is dark, the moon is pale,
The light shines on the sea;
The cool wind's breath brings shivers to
The man who will not be.

The mud now soft from torrential rain
Grips his ankles tightly,
But he is enraged and out of touch,
Fearful and struggling mightily.

These woods that lie so soft and wet
Loom dark before the eyes
Of he who is long used to gloom
And is with life surprised:

So dark, so still, so full of fear
A wet, cold night appears
To one who seeks his life in things
And counts it up in years.

He's going home and soon is gone,
Past this arduous path.
What home is this the blind man seeks
That binds his life in wrath?

The poem was wwritten 3-15-1967, age 19, when I decided to change my college major from premed to just pure biology. The poem was originally titled, "On Changing Majors." But there seems to be much more going on in the poem than just that. What was I really thinking about?

Abraham

Father of faith, compatriot now,
A short year past the unleaved shoot
Thorned with suspicion your faithful bow:
Beauty not apparent could only be mute.

Emotions, insight, experience and power,
Feverish delusions have softened and cooled.
The budded sprout begins to flower
In myriad life, where intellect ruled.

Countryman! Let us struggle hard:
Submission is gone, and likewise flight.
Trembling and hesitant, be on our guard
Together and unknown to sight.

The fallen fortress a palace then seems
And ivory tower the bower of dreams.

Conversion

For four long years I sought for God
And four years more denied him; yet
If death be near in fear alone,
Death it is that guides me now
To faith long sought and long denied.
For fear recalls the repressed prayer
And truth appears to leap despair:
This coward's heart with joy fears God.

Written in 1974, after a cold night on the mountain with my friends. I don't recall the details but something literally put the "fear of God" in me that night.

Honesty

Life comes in times of crisis.
It stops of a moment and asks,
Who are you?
What do you love?
What will you die for?

Peace and contentment are blessings,
They have no price,
They are not for sale.
I would not die for them,
I will not live for them.

I do not even seek these blessings.
They are simple gifts
To be enjoyed in happy times.
Honesty is not just a better way,
It is the only way.

The poem was written September 12, 1974. Many years later, in 2011, I used this poem as part of a commencement speech at Boston Children's Hospital, in which I encouraged the graduates to listen to their hearts and to follow their conscience.

Uncertainty

There are many ways I see tonight
Divergent and converging around me
(But no solace, no consolation,
No restful respite, no sharing pain).
I choose alone a doubtful choice,
My being bound by its beckoning:
You who cannot guide my life
In ways a man can understand
Must guide me as I make this choice.

I Need a Hole to Get Sick In

I need a hole to get sick in.
You bleat about nature
As if it were some kind of Eden,
Peaceful, innocent and perfect,
And we but fat, contented sheep,
Eating, vomiting and chewing our cud.
In this, you hit the mark:
The more I hear, the more I need
To vomit on your scenery.

Do you think I understand it?
The chair that lies across the room
(Where I hurled it)
Doesn't understand.
Was I angry then?
No, not at anything
(Yes, at everything)

Memories of the Tree

Breast-piercing wound,
All bloody with love and hate,
O friend and lover---
What lies are these,
Who yearns your pain to salve suffering,
Whence this unmanly love?

Draw forth the dagger,
Devil-damned drawn dart,
The arrow ally!
Build me, grow me,
Bleed to my roots,
That there of your strength
I may drink deeply.

The poem was originally written in the spring of 1970 and titled, "To Those, Over the Years" but I cannot recall now if it refers to anyone in particular. I renamed it in 1976 as a metaphor for conversion and faith, using the tree as a reference to the cross.

Relativities

The trees rebuked me, called me foolish.
"You are ignorant," I replied,
Walking further on my way.

The street was long but I arrived
And said to all the buildings there,
"You are ugly."

They replied and said to me,
"If you knew what you were talking about,
You would love us, too."

"Go to Hell," I said, departing.
"Do I care if you are blind?
No one else can speak for me."

My ugliness is now your truth,
Your truth becomes my beauty,
My beauty your damned foolishness.

We swim in urine, blood and semen
And ask no questions of the world.
If we argue, we agree.

The poem was written 1-21-1971 when I was 23 years old. Although I did not realize it at the time, it is very loosely related to 1 Corinthians 1:18-25:

For the message of the cross is foolishness to those who are perishing, but to us who are being saved it is the power of God. For it is written: "I will destroy the wisdom of the wise; the intelligence of the intelligent I will frustrate." Where is the wise person? Where is the teacher of the law? Where is the philosopher of this age? Has not God made foolish the wisdom of the world? For since in the wisdom of God the world through its wisdom did not know him, God was pleased through the foolishness of what was preached to save those who believe. Jews demand signs and Greeks look for wisdom, but we preach Christ crucified: a stumbling block to Jews and foolishness to Gentiles, but to those whom God has called, both Jews and Greeks, Christ the power of God and the wisdom of God. For the foolishness of God is wiser than human wisdom, and the weakness of God is stronger than human strength.

The Easy Mistress

She wakes in the morning early with me
And claims my empty, refreshed mind,
Returns me from my wandering,
While in that touch so gentle on me
Seizing with complete possession
The life to her I have surrendered:

> Her touch is easy, imperceptible,
> And holds me like a spider's web.

I gave myself completely to her
In that first infatuation
Of a heedless and romantic time;
Four years past, it is the same
And tangled inextricably,
Like a fly she sucks me dry.

> Fattened from my years' attentions,
> She leaves me withered, barren, hollow.

Love left this union years ago;
Loathe to leave her spider bed
And loathsome weak remaining there,
Each day I find it ever easier
To take her in a cold embrace
And promise away the fruit of the day.

Ruthless with my paralysis,
The bitch-mistress is destroying me.

Whew! Intense angst! I am still not sure what it means. The poem was written 10-29-1975 when I was in the midst of a spiritual crisis. The mistress is metaphorical, not real.

The Tribute
(Inspired by Shaffer's "Equus")

Upon what blood-stained altar
Of human sacrifice
Where the beating heart is torn
From the living, breathing breast

And in what holy fire
Where the holocaust is burned
As the white smoke rises
To merge the midnight mist

Lies the dying offering
Bleeding and ablaze,
Pleasing to the fearsome god
Consuming life to rule the dead?

Heart of fantasy and fear!
Running with the foxes
To endless caves of dreams
Of snakes and nakedness,

Screaming to be heard
Against an angry god,
Almighty God the Father
In the caverns of the mind,

Lie silent on the stone.
The entrails are augured
And the sacrifice consumed
To illuminate the night.

The altar now is empty,
Drained of blood and cold.
Order is restored and
Darkness rules the world.

And yet there are some times
When a furtive passion moves
Past the bare and bloodless altar
And the sleeping ancient god

With incandescent dreams
Of foxes in the night
And insects singing to the earth
The worship of the world,

And in those magic moments
A thousand burning lives cry out,
Celebrating joy and pain
In the face of fire and death.

Dirge for Memorial Day

A fog-warning mournful throaty horn
Like muffled punctual clockwork sounds,
Muscling over obscured water---
Ponderous heartbeat of the harbor
Throbbing a thirty-second sequence,
Moving past pier-bound fisherman
Sleepily staring, mindlessly quiet,
Past pier and beach looking, waiting,
For rising foggy recollections
Of fellow soldiers, dead friends
For whom a taut and brooding horn
Limns the memories of living lost.

Now comes thunder-sent torrential rain
Drenching the windswept shadowy marsh,
Distant depths dark and obscure
Across the roiled and steaming water,
Lightning-lit untimely evening
Morbid and heavy over the land---
The ghostly battle of earth and sky
Conjuring up to consciousness
The loving living's undying dead,
As if their spirits came to call
Contending fiercely with creation.

With such tribute on Memorial Day
A sea-dark beauty sadly reigns;
The world is not a picture postcard.

The poem was written in 1976 at Harbor Beach, Michigan, and on the road from Bay City to Saginaw traveling on highway M-13.

John's Place

My name is Daniel.
That is what the English called me.
My real name is Takawanbpait.
I lived in the place by the river
Where the water goes over the rocks.
My people have been here forever,
Since the Great Spirit brought us here.
The English call us Indians,
But we have never been to India.
We are the people,
Wampanoags of the Algonquin clan,
And this is our home.

A man rode into our village one day.
He was English but he spoke our language
(not very well, but we could talk).
He said his name was John,
And that he brought good news from the Great Spirit.
He said that we are all children of the Great Spirit.
He said that many years ago,
The Great Spirit came and lived with his People
And taught them to love one another
As brothers and sisters do.
He said that another man named John
Said that we should be like that, too,
That we should love all of the Peoples here,
The English, and even the Pequots.

We built a place for John to talk
Whenever he came to visit our village.
When we gathered together in John's place,
He said the Great Spirit was there, too,
And helped us welcome all of the People.
John taught me to talk there, too,
And I continued when he was gone.
They said we were the praying Indians.
We said we were the people of the Great Spirit.

But now my People are all gone,
Our bodies are lying in the ground.
Other Peoples came to John's place,
Black people from a place called Africa,
White people from a place called Ireland.
John's place welcomed all of them.

Then John's place moved, away from the river,
To another place near our burying ground.
I went to see this place.
I saw a strange flag flying there.
It looked like the rainbows we used to see
When sunlight chased the rain away.
They said the flag is like that, too,
Chasing fear away, and hate.
They said the flag means all are welcome,
All the Peoples of the rainbow
Who gather there like we did
In our village long ago.

John and I belong in this place.

This is still our home.

The poem was written for the First Congregational Church of Natick, Massachusetts, which was founded by the Reverend John Eliot in 1651 as a place where Native Americans who had converted to Christianity could gather to pray. The church now flies the rainbow flag over its door to signal that it is still "John's Place" and still welcomes everyone no matter what.

The Flint

A Gospel or a Psalm

The earth was once a formless void,
There was darkness on the deep (1),
When Light that was the light of men (2)
Commenced to move across the water,
A light with which to conquer darkness (3),
A sparking flint igniting things.

Resentful darkness, seeing the light,
Schemed to kill it so darkness might live
(For aided by evil (4), each man kills
The thing he loves (5), so he must die).
Then darkness owned the hearts of men
Who hate and fight and kill each other.

Do not despair to see light die!
Light took flesh and dwells among us (6),
Present in our hearts like flint,
Showering sparks of love renewed.
Strike the flint again, my brother,
See the light leap up within,
Drive out fear (7) and lead us to
Adventures in the Light of love.

He who lives in love
Forever lives in light
Shining in the darkness,
Light lives on in him.

REFERENCES:

1. Genesis 1: 2
2. John 1: 4
3. John 1: 5
4. Genesis 3: 1-7
5. "Ballad of Reading Gaol," Oscar Wilde
6. John 1: 14
7. 1 John 4: 18
8. "Reasons of the Heart," John S. Dunne
9. 1 John 4: 16

"At times our own light goes out and is rekindled by a spark from another person. Each of us has cause to think with deep gratitude of those who have lighted the flame within us."---Albert Schweitzer

On Re-Reading Philosophy

How simple it seemed so long ago,
When virtues could be named and counted
And ideas sounded like common sense,

To search for certain truth and beauty
In dreams of perfect human love
And deeds that make a difference!

What is the point of life on earth?
Why do we live, work, love and die,
And what of it all will we leave behind?

The answers are not so easy now
That passing years have only left
Uncertain ambiguities,

Still waiting for the situation
Needing a profound response,
A watershed of strength and will.

Abortive Spring

Promise of summer, in rejoicing born
(Slumbering now in icy seclusion),
A premature and desperate delusion
Convulsed with joy the winter-torn.

Beauty, ecstatic imagination
Engendered dreams in frolic and mirth
When nature triumphant announced her rebirth
To the bugling trumpets of men's admiration.

Not long in life, but soon harassed
By winter's vengeful last contortion,
The aborted hope, raised out of proportion,
Relinquished life and breathed its last.

Ancient Friends

In the childhood of the modern gods who loiter in the sunlight,
Swaggering through ruined temples from age to age,
Armored in knowable virtue, two bronzed friends walked together arm in
hand.
How much it was to them, and how sufficient
To have from the other the promise each knew was enough!
Moss grows in their footsteps now, between the saplings
Thrust between the stones to bring them down;
Fields to their eyes became forests
Cut for cities built where friends once walked.
But the air they breathed, the starlit sky above,
The rock-strewn mountain pathways leading to the sea
Are as they were when that was all.
There are no altars in the temple of Hephaestion.

Body Song

Come now, let us celebrate,
Celebrate the body,
Wander in its wonderment,
Overwhelming body.

Look into the crystal eyes
That magnify the body,
See the man whose life is there
Reflected in his body.

The vintage of our life on earth
Experienced by the body
Is poured out when we pause to share
Soul's passage through the body.

My notes for this poem state that it was written "vaguely with reference to
my friends at Notre Dame" when I was a student there. I was also reading
Walt Whitman at the time.

Carl Hamblin, 1968
(With Apologies to Edgar Lee Masters)

The press of our local paper was wrecked
And I was abused and beaten
For publishing this on the day Dr. King was murdered in Memphis:

"I saw a bald eagle, wrapped in a flag,
Perched on the shoulders of its patriarch.
A great multitude passed in front of them,
Shouting and cheering and striking one another.
In his left hand the patriarch held a gun.
He was brandishing the gun,
Killing now a black man, his starving child,
A compassionate youth, and now a prophet.
In his right hand was a supper plate,
Into which the crowd tossed money and meat
To feed the vicious, hungry bird.
The national patriarch pronounced to his people:
"Behold, here is the guardian of democracy."
Then a man wearing a worker's cap
Leapt and snatched the eagle's flag.
With dexterous fingers he fashioned a noose,
And the people became a massing lynch mob.
Chanting their national songs and anthems,
They seized a black man and hung him high,
And trampled those who reached out to stop them.

The madness of a dying nation
Was written in their race---
And the world saw why they worshipped the eagle."

This poem is a re-imagining of Masters' classic poem, which was written after the Haymarket riots and the execution of the anarchists there on November 11, 1887.

CARL HAMBLIN
BY EDGAR LEE MASTERS 1868–1950

The press of the Spoon River *Clarion* was wrecked,
And I was tarred and feathered,
For publishing this on the day the Anarchists were hanged in Chicago:
"I saw a beautiful woman with bandaged eyes
Standing on the steps of a marble temple.
Great multitudes passed in front of her,
Lifting their faces to her imploringly.
In her left hand she held a sword.
She was brandishing the sword,
Sometimes striking a child, again a laborer,
Again a slinking woman, again a lunatic.
In her right hand she held a scale;
Into the scale pieces of gold were tossed
By those who dodged the strokes of the sword.
A man in a black gown read from a manuscript:
'She is no respecter of persons.'
Then a youth wearing a red cap
Leaped to her side and snatched away the bandage.
And lo, the lashes had been eaten away
From the oozy eye-lids;
The eye-balls were seared with a milky mucus;
The madness of a dying soul
Was written on her face i
But the multitude saw why she wore the bandage."

Interlude

And so, and so, the time has come
To think about a world of things.

In a mountain hollow thistle blooms
Along the meadow looking south
From Mabry's empty timber cabin.
What is time to what is timeless?
Death is the beginning of philosophy.

Like thistle, leaning back and silent,
Ending a quarrel with the centuries,
My mind dissolves in Smokies sunlight.

Lake Michigan

Warm sand, a quiet sun,
And bird calls; the sentient wind
Adds harmony and moves the sounds---

A noiseless symphony of nature aroused,
Apparent source of being, perceived,
Dialectic of all that is.

Night

Soft, cold, pregnant and possible,
A mist, sufficient to wet, brisk-breeze-bathed,
Suffuses the lamplight in shadow
Within opacity, making air organic,
Sufficing (almost) to excite things.

The mist exists, in that it rains;
Conjoins a torrent through mind, a man,
A scepter-sprinkled Earth---by it all.
It wets in silence the warm frozen grass
And cleans the night in freshness.

Between the man and the mist
The axe (the Cross adz) cannot fall:
Today is not a time for executions.
(God in heaven and to hell with hell)
Now is to drink deep-draught-daring.

The debt to Gerard Manley Hopkins is obvious. The poem was written January 29, 1969 when I was a 21 year old senior at the University of Notre Dame. It was inspired by a walk across the campus in the mist one night.

Sunday

A deep-down sense of sameness tonight,
My life seen in a television screen
Tuned until a merciful bedtime.
If I turn it off, there is nothing.

Time steals my life
In routines I make for myself.
For excitement today
I have but to change the channel,
Discover yesterday's adventure
Ready to be relived.
I know all the programs.

Like every Sunday of the year
Spent in search of distraction,
I throw the day away with my life.

Unfinished Business

Warmed by the high Sierra sunlight,
The snow melts in the pines above
And pelts a cool rain down upon me,
Smiling at my urban adventure
Among the people of the night.

Sequoias, stand and speak your mind!
You tell me what a fool I am?
It was nothing, unfinished business,
An unlamented, unrepented
Careless adventure of passing youth.

Adrift with other people's passions,
Rootless, trapped and vulnerable,
I cannot live in crowded cities
Like where I was, they make me crazy
Bringing out the worst in me.

But resting here begins to clear
My mind of yesterday's confusion
Between my self and my desire,
Granite rocks and giant redwoods
Raising my song of consciousness.

The Mirror

Image grim imagined there,
Formless as a misty fog
Forfending future mystery,

Stranger, close and clear approach,
Strength and solitude encroach,
Within the sanctuary, come:

Pure in shape and delicate,
Litanies of life and death
Sleeping long now wake enchanted,

Chanting songs and secrets, blazing
Beatific in your eyes.
O stranger, see! For you are me.

The Bicentennial
(July 4,1976)

"Break out the flags, strike up the band,
Light up the sky," the President said.
No meaningful things were done all day.

Many were the celebrations,
Tall ships, fireworks and parades,
Everyone doing what they knew best.

(Some friends who knew what was to come
Went to the woods to escape it all;
The land is ours, but we are the land's.)

I fixed my bike and took a ride
And went canoeing in the rain;
It was a proper day to start anew.

I tried to do a lot of things
And dream of doing many more,
Singing today the gift of myself.

When I Became a Pacifist

Life, beating from a shell, is distant, hollow.
There it is, from far away it moves a listless man,
Bent, bowed, not broken, birthing a savage plan,
A brutal resolve: no one through me will follow

The shrouded path of sorrow. Intense rage so brief:
Is this the grief of a stricken soul who knows
Of death, or the fury that of a sudden grows,
From passion leaps when the numbing cloud of grief

Is swept away? Bitter anger! This it is,
Thus: The murky darkness of senseless fate
Veil-like lifts abrupt---in memories that are his
Reveals a precious, close and priceless rare estate.

This anger, its own cause and own effect,
Will one day lessen: time corrects.

The poem was written on February 9, 1968 in memory of John Moore, a friend who died December 17, 1967 at 23 years of age. His death made me realize how precious life is and convinced me that I could never take that life away from another person.

The Storyteller
An Apostrophe to Literature

Sit down here inside the circle,
Storyteller, sit with us,
Tell us tales of terror and joy,

Amuse and entertain our guests
Who gather here to greet you now,
Anxious in anticipation,

For every moral has a story,
Every man his motive myth
That tells him who he truly is.

Of epic heroes seeking truth
And meaning in adventure,
Recite the legends.

Of ambitious men consumed with pride
And doomed men who struggle on,
Teach us of fate.

Of innocent men who suffer for love
That conquers evil in the end,
Speak of the cross.

Every story speaks to my heart
But one alone can bring me peace.
Sing to my soul.

Part Four
Youthful Intimations

A CHILD'S VIEW OF NATURE, FAITH AND SPIRITUALITY

When the Wind Comes

The wind is gruff,
It blows in rough,
It may seem tough,
   But it's majestic.

Its' splendor is great,
You cannot debate,
Nor can you rate
   It's power.

And as it blows,
Everyone knows
Its' power shows
   It's grace.

Written January, 1960, when I was 12 years old. I think this was my first poem. It is interesting that my first poem as a child was about nature, which has been my inspiration all of my life. And grace! What does a 12 year old boy know about grace?

The Summer Storm

One warm sunny day
When everything was fine,
I saw far distant
A rough gray line.

The line I soon learned
Meant an oncoming storm.
The weather bureau said
It was beginning to form.

By the first ray of dawn
It would be well here,
And already the thunder
Was scaring the deer.

When I woke up,
It was right above,
Birds had found refuge
Like the robin and the dove.

And in a few minutes,
The storm began,
It far surpassed anything
Made by man.

The lightning and rain
Were lovely to see,

The heavens had opened
Majestically.

The storm was long
And lasted for an hour;
The animals were scared,
Within they did cower.

When the sun came out,
It was great to be alive,
The animals ran about
And the bees left their hive.

The storm is over now
But it left its mark
As I walk along the spongy ground
And listen to the lark.

The handwriting in the pencil version of this poem is very immature, almost certainly from junior high school or earlier. I am guessing 7th or 8th grade, maybe around age 13.

The Jaybird

The Jay is a bird not well liked,
It's good deeds are almost unknown;
But this much I can say
For the little blue jay,
It does have a little renown.

The Bird actually starts with its' feathered chest,
I'm sure that everyone knows it;
The beak is long
And like a prong,
And does he ever like to show it!

The Bird is a multitude of pretty colors,
Among these blue, purple and white;
Each one shows
The Jay Bird knows
How to make himself visible at night.

When the little Jay dies,
'Tis a sad matter indeed;
And if the Blue Jay
Should die in May
Something happy is what the month needs.

The very thing I fear to say,
I suppose that you want to know;
And this is it
(You'd better sit),
He's a bully when the wind doth blow.

The poem is undated but clearly immature, and based on my handwriting at the time, most likely written when I was 13 years old.

Written During Blackness

Drearily the visage of Nature
Extends her gloomy countenance of grey
Across our world.
And equally as dreary
Become the visages of mankind,
Their despair unfurled.

Nowhere in this view is seen
The cheerful, vivifying orb of light
We call the Sun;
Visible nowhere is the ethereal nature
Of Nature herself in her grandest glory---
Beauty undone.

The sun says, it's Spring today,
Yet in the same vein denies herself:
Spring is not this!
Is Spring morose and cheerless,
Dark and sunless as thus she appears;
Is nature amiss?

Words too pale to describe this
We use as our limit of description
For this kind of day.
Man knows none more dreary,
Less cheery, which he could utilize
To explain it away.

But perhaps it is only some futility
Which man possesses within his nature,
Unexpressed;
And perhaps this is the reason
Why he stands thus, dreary and despairing,
And distressed.

Maybe it is not Nature that fails:
The darkness may be created by ourselves,
Solaces's art;
If we strive to defeat it
And assume the countenance of gaiety,
Despair may depart!

So he struggles against himself,
Becomes cheerful---and lo! He beholds
The glory of Spring!
Nature was waiting for man to change---
She knew that she is only what each one makes her,
And stands, rejoicing!

This is a complex poem, written at the end of my senior year in high school. It is dated May 28, 1965, when I was 17 years old.

The Ballad of Bonnie Prince Charlie
Or The Stuart Invasion of 1745

Bonnie Prince Charlie has come from France
To free his homeland, Scotland dear,
To free Great Britain from Hanover's rule.
"The Stuarts are back! Charles Edward is here!"

Edward will avenge the Stuarts,
Edward will regain the throne.
Landing in the outer islands,
With nary a follower, nearly alone,

He marched to Scotland's capital,
To Edinburgh, his native home,
While 'round him rallied the highland clans
To fight the British on Scottish loam.

King George then mustered all the British
Trying to halt the princely heir,
But Charles took Edinburgh from the German
And held once more all Scotland fair.

The British might marched north to Scotland
To engage the Pretender in deadly war,
But Hanover ran at Prestonpan
And opened to Charles, England's door.

So Charles invaded England great.
Through the lowlands Edward went,
Across the border, over the Cheviots,
He led his mighty regiment.

The British army retreated back
Until Culloden Moor they passed.
There Charles met George in bloody strife;
The battle raged furious, hot and fast.

Neither side could tell who'd won---
The smoke and din obscured the fray,
But when it cleared, the field revealed
The Stuart cause had lost the day.

The Scots had run, the Scots had fled,
Charles Edward's cause was clearly done.
Never again would Stuart threaten;
The chase for Edward was begun.

O'er hill, o'er vale the Stuart went,
He fled to Scotland and the clans,
For there he figured he'd be safe---
A fugitive in dear Scotland.

George was secure on England's throne,
While Charles was like the stag in the chase.
The Scots held safe their vanquished Charles,
While through their land he ran the race.

The loyal Jacobites, still his friends,
Sheltered him and gave him rest.
But close on his heels, wherever he went,
Relentlessly, the English pressed.

He fled then to the outer islands,
The place from which he made his start.
The chase drew close, he had to hide
By wall, by tower, in carriage and cart.

He sailed soon for the Continent,
To France, where he thought he would be free;
But France agreed to exile the Stuarts,
And Edward died in Italy.

Over ten-score years have passed
Since Charles invaded England great;
Naught remains of the Stuart cause
'Cept memories to ruminate.

A wonderful poem! I loved it at the time and my teacher asked me to read it out loud in front of my 9th grade English class in the spring of 1962. My teacher thought it was great, too. I was 14 years old at the time and a huge fan of Walter Scott.

Part Five
Four Sermons and a Story

A Franciscan Walk in the Woods

A Sermon Given at the First Congregational Church in Natick,
Massachusetts
October 9, 2011

I am here today to talk about experiencing the glory of God's creation through the vision of Saint Francis of Assisi. And it is a beautiful day today, a great day to celebrate the world that God created. I was originally scheduled to give this talk on August 28, which was the day of the hurricane, a day when nature challenged our relationship to creation. The worship service was cancelled that day, and so we rescheduled, and we could not have wished for a better day than today.

When my pastor invited me to give this reflection, we wanted to talk about nature before the end of the summer. The hurricane changed that plan, but perhaps the ideas here will help us experience more fully the glory of our New England autumn. I am very grateful for the opportunity to share them with you and hope that these ideas will be interesting to you and will help all of us to experience nature in a new way through the vision of Francis of Assisi.

These ideas came to me while I was on vacation in upstate New York last year. For summer reading I had picked up a book about the life of Francis of Assisi. There is much to admire about Francis, but I was particularly interested in his approach to nature. Another book I read described Francis's approach as a form of nature mysticism. The idea came to me to try to see if I might be able to experience nature much as Francis might have done. So I got up early one morning and went for a walk in the woods in the state park that is next to the community where we have our cottage. I entered the woods at 7:00 AM Monday morning on a bright, sunny summer day and pretty much had the trail all to myself at that hour. As I was walking, I kept repeating to myself, "When I walk the woods with Francis, Francis shows my God to me." And over the course of the next several hours spent with him in the woods, he did indeed do just that. Along the way, and by doing so, he helped me to identify several principles that I think might help others have a similar experience. I tested these ideas later on a few more walks in the woods, last year and again this summer, either by myself or with a friend, and thought that this might be a good time to share them with you.

I think that a good way to start on a <u>Franciscan Walk in the Woods</u> is to recite Francis' great poem, the "Canticle of the Sun." Francis composed this poem in the last two years of his life, finishing the final stanzas literally on his deathbed, a few days before he died. As such, it is both an introduction and a summary of his thinking about God and nature. Let us recite it now. When I was in the woods with a friend, we began our walk by reciting it out loud, speaking to the natural world we were about to engage. We alternated reading the stanzas on that occasion, and I would like for us to do pretty much the same thing today. So let's read it out loud.

(Recite the Canticle given below)

At this point, when I am in the woods, either alone or with a friend, I like to start my walk with Francis with a prayer to God who created all of us and all of nature. There is no particular text, just a personal prayer of praise and a request for inspiration as we immerse ourselves in nature. But the point here is to pray in a very different way than what we are used to in church. Rather than bending over and bowing my head, as I might do in church, I like to pray to the God of creation with my head thrown back and my arms outstretched, opening myself up to all of the experiences that will come. Indeed, I'll pray like this pretty much anytime I am outdoors, on a golf course or at the end of a workday when I come home and look up at the sky.

Having grounded oneself in Francis's great poem of praise and prayed to God for inspiration, it is time to begin the walk. At this point I would like to suggest a few general principles that I have found to be useful in the walks I have taken.

First, one must slow down. The destination is not important. When I was walking on a trail in a state park that led eventually to a nature center, I realized that it was not important whether I ever got there or not. The only destination that counts is God, and God can be found all around us, in the woods or anywhere else we may be. Thus, when we are walking in the woods, we do not need to worry about where we are going or when we will get there, as long as we are moving closer to God.

Second, one must try not to name things. Naming is a way of controlling things and thus a way of exerting power over nature. This is the opposite of what Francis would intend. Francis would see all of nature as God's creation, as we are, to be loved by us because God created it. Thus the only power we should exert in nature is the power of God's love. Rather than naming trees, plants, animals, insects, etc. as the guidebooks would have us do, we should instead address them in the terms that Francis would have used, as he did in the "Canticle of the Sun," and also in the "Sermon to the Birds" and other writings. On my walk I encountered and addressed Brother Moth, Sister Ant, Brother Chipmunk, Father Owl, and Mother Tree. Using the language of love, as we would in our family, reminds us that we are all parts of God's creation.

Third, one should try to look at, smell, touch, see and feel everything going on in nature. By using all of our senses we can immerse ourselves completely in God's creation. This was a radical notion in Francis's time, and remains so in our time. Rather than trying to distance ourselves from the reality of our senses, as we might during solitary meditation, this Franciscan approach seeks to place us securely within the reality of God's creation. This is part of the nature mysticism that Francis practiced and taught. Most of the time when we walk in the woods, we look only at what is in front of us, or do not pay attention to what is going on because we are thinking about something else. The idea here is to focus on all of our senses, not on our thoughts, and to try to experience everything that is going on all around us, in front, above, behind, nearby and in the distance.

I do not know if it is possible to open up one's self to the spiritual senses, as well as to the physical senses, during a walk in the woods. But it is worth a try. Can we find the spirit of God moving in what we find in Nature all around us? Can we find the spirit of God in the people who are with us, either physically (people who are on the walk with us) or spiritually (people we love or have loved in the past)? Perhaps we can at least open up our spiritual senses to such a possibility by praying, "Come, Holy Spirit, show me the way."

Fourth, one should stop frequently, bend down and look carefully at what is happening on the ground. So much of nature happens at levels we never experience, such as underground or in the sea, but it is there nonetheless as God created it. Getting close to the ground helps us to see things that we might not appreciate otherwise when we are walking upright. I think it is especially important to look for the smallest, most insignificant thing one can find on the ground, such as an ant scurrying across the path or a tiny wildflower blooming close to the ground. The idea here is to appreciate and celebrate the fact that God does not love any less that which is the least of all creation. The giant tree or the eagle soaring in the air is not greater than the tiny ant on the ground. All were created by God and we should give praise to God for all of them.

Of course, this is also the message of the Gospel. In Matthew 6:25-33, Jesus teaches us that God created the birds in the sky and the lilies in the field and loves and cares for them without regard for their value to others. God created us, too, and we should place our faith and trust in God to love and care for us without regard for our value to others.

I told you that when I went into the woods to walk with Francis of Assisi, I prayed for inspiration and understanding. It was at this point that I was literally struck down by a sudden insight that sent me to my knees on the trail in the woods. It was not quite a Pauline "on the road to Damascus" type of moment, but you get the idea. I realized that if God loves the tiny ant as much as God loves the soaring eagle, then surely God must love the weakest human being as much as God loves the president or the pope. The child with profound disabilities, the adult with dementia, the person living in a vegetative state, is loved by God as much as we are, and we should recognize, celebrate and share God's love with all of them. I am a pediatric neurologist and these are my patients, so the insight that sent me to my knees was the realization that I must look for the spirit of God living in them and help others to see how much they are loved by God. This is what I am now trying to do.

Fifth, the whole idea here is to find joy in everything. The stories tell us that Francis preached to the birds, but I suspect he also listened to what the birds were saying to him. And I think the birds were saying, "Be joyful for everything God has created and find comfort in being a part of it." If we pause to look at a wildflower, let us just say, "How beautiful!" If we hear a bird call in the distance, let us just say, "How lovely!" Indeed, this spiritual joy is another key to the nature mysticism that Francis practiced and taught. I believe that when we walk the woods with Francis as our guide, we will be able to experience this spiritual joy in all of God's creation. And this joy is sufficient for us.

In Matthew 6: 34, Jesus says, "Each day has enough trouble of its own." When we put our faith and trust in God, the joy that comes is sufficient to get us through the day. My hope is that when we walk in the woods with Francis as our guide, perhaps following the ideas I have outlined here, we will be able to experience and celebrate something of this joy that comes from God and can be found in all of God's creation. And I do believe that this joy can be a force for healing the troubles of our lives and for strengthening our faith.

Thank you for listening to what I have said today and I look forward to walking together with you in the future.

REFERENCES

House, A. <u>Francis of Assisi: A Revolutionary Life</u>. HiddenSpring, Mahwah, NJ, 2001.

Sorrell, R.D. <u>Saint Francis of Assisi and Nature</u>. New York: Oxford University Press, 1988.

THE CANTICLE OF THE SUN
by Francis of Assisi

Most high, all powerful, all good Lord! All praise is yours, all glory, all honor, and all blessing. To you, alone, Most High, do they belong. No mortal lips are worthy to pronounce your name.

Be praised, my Lord, through all your creatures, especially through my lord Brother Sun, who brings the day; and you give light through him. And he is beautiful and radiant in all his splendor! Of you, Most High, he bears the likeness.

Be praised, my Lord, through Sister Moon and the stars; in the heavens you have made them, precious and beautiful.

Be praised, my Lord, through Brothers Wind and Air, and clouds and storms, and all the weather, through which you give your creatures sustenance.

Be praised, My Lord, through Sister Water; she is very useful, and humble, and precious, and pure.

Be praised, my Lord, through Brother Fire, through whom you brighten the night. He is beautiful and cheerful, and powerful and strong.

Be praised, my Lord, through our sister Mother Earth, who feeds us and rules us, and produces various fruits with colored flowers and herbs.

Be praised, my Lord, through those who forgive for love of you; through those who endure sickness and trial. Happy those who endure in peace, for by you, Most High, they will be crowned.

Be praised, my Lord, through our Sister Bodily Death, from whose embrace no living person can escape. Woe to those who die in mortal sin! Happy those she finds doing your most holy will. The second death can do no harm to them.

Praise and bless my Lord, and give thanks, and serve him with great humility.

A Science of Good and Evil

A Sermon Given at the First Congregational Church in Natick,
Massachusetts
July 25, 2014

INTRODUCTION

Good morning. I am honored by the opportunity to talk to you and to reflect on the scripture readings we have just heard. I am especially honored to be able to do so with my wife, my sister and her two daughters present. This may be my best opportunity to show them that their uncle is pretty cool. I also want to thank my pastor for allowing me to share these ideas with you.

If God is good, why does evil exist? That is the question I want to address today. We need only to look at the news headlines every day to realize that evil clearly does exist in our world. Vladimir Putin, the Prime Minister of Russia, shamelessly conquers and annexes an independent Crimea, and then threatens the independence of Ukraine. A severely disturbed racist young man in Charleston, South Carolina, shoots and kills a Black pastor and several members of the congregation. Islamic terrorists slaughter innocent civilians in Syria, Iraq and Nigeria. We can add many more stories to this list. Why does God allow these terrible things to happen? Or (from a different perspective), does God really allow it, or does it just happen?

Another way to think about this is to imagine that Satan, the devil, makes these evil things happen. Perhaps Putin, the Charleston shooter, the ISIS terrorists, are all possessed by the devil, and that is why they do what they do. We know from the Bible that the people of that time clearly thought that the devil did exist. The Bible says that Jesus himself was tempted by the devil. Many of us were brought up on lurid stories of the

Archangel Michael fighting Lucifer for control of Heaven, and eventually driving the devil down into Hell. But there is a subtle problem with this image. It is almost as if there is a good God, Yahweh or the God of our Christian Trinity, on the one hand, and an evil God, the devil Satan, on the other hand. And this could imply a kind of pantheism, a belief in multiple gods. Certainly many people in biblical times believed in multiple gods, some good and some bad. Roman and Greek society had many such gods, and so did the other peoples of the Middle East. Indeed, the great accomplishment of the prophet Muhammed was to end the common Arab belief in multiple gods and to proclaim, "There is no God but Allah."

Today, I want to ask, is it possible to account for the presence of evil in our world without having to imagine the presence of a separate evil force? Do we need to accept a cosmic battle between good and evil? Or is our belief in a "God-Who-Is-Love" (as described by the apostle John) sufficient for us to understand why evil exists?

Now here comes the tough part. I also want to ask, is it possible that science can help us to answer these questions?

THERMODYNAMICS

I majored in biology and chemistry in college and enjoyed every course I took, maybe with one exception. I got an A in all of my classes except for my class in physical chemistry, where I was lucky to get a B. It was a tough class. The class average on the first exam was 35 (out of a possible 100). But one thing I learned there, and that I want to share with you today, was how physical energy is managed in our world. Once I explain that, I will try to draw an analogy with how spiritual energy is managed in our world as well.

I realize this is summer vacation and no one wants to think very hard, but please allow me to describe what are known in physical chemistry as the three laws of thermodynamics.

The <u>first law</u> states that, "Energy can neither be created nor destroyed. It can only change forms." For example, solar energy can be changed to heat or electricity, but the total amount of energy remains the same. At least, this is true for our earthly world. But, if the universe is infinite, then the total amount of energy in the universe would be infinite, too. By analogy, then, the spiritual energy of an infinite universe created by God may also be infinite.

The <u>second law</u> states that, "The entropy of an isolated system not in equilibrium will increase over time and reach its maximal value at equilibrium," This is a much more difficult concept. Let me try to explain. Entropy is a measure of disorder or chaos. Thus, unless something happens, all natural things will tend to fall apart and move toward disorder or chaos. Energy needs to be added in order to prevent this descent into chaos.

Okay, that is pretty dense. Like I said, I only got a B in the course. Let's think of it as being like a garden, like the gardens many of us have planted this summer. If we just leave the garden alone, the tomatoes and the weeds will all grow up together and choke each other out. But if we go into the garden from time to time and pull out the weeds, and maybe add a little fertilizer and some water when needed, the tomatoes will thrive. It takes energy, our energy, to make our garden strong. Keep this in mind, since I will come back to it later when I will refer to verses from Matthew's gospel.

The <u>third law</u> states that the condition of complete equilibrium, when there is no order or structure at all, exists only at absolute zero temperature, which is the coldest possible temperature of all. We'll hold off on thinking about that for now, but keep it in mind, too, since it will have some possible significance later when we think about the management of spiritual energy.

THE QUESTION

From our knowledge of these thermodynamic laws about how the physical energy of God's creation works, can we derive an understanding or insight into God's spiritual laws about how our human life on earth works? More specifically, do these scientific laws provide a way to understand why evil exists in a world that God has committed to good?

SOME INSPIRATIONS

In Matthew 13:24-30, Jesus describes how wheat and weeds can grow together in a garden, but at the harvest, they will be separated, and the weeds will burn while the wheat is brought into the barn. One implication (described in Matthew 13:36-43) is that good people (like the wheat) will be saved, while evil people (like the weeds) will be destroyed and burn in Hell. However, another way of reading this is that in the gardens of our soul, we have both wheat and weeds growing together. In other words, we have both good and evil present in us together, and it is up to us to harvest the wheat and extinguish the weeds in our souls. And it takes the infusion of spiritual energy in order to do so.

This idea also resonates with something Alexander Solzhenitsyn once wrote: "If only it were all so simple! If only there were evil people some-where insidiously committing evil deeds, and it were necessary only to separate them from the rest of us and destroy them. But the line dividing good and evil cuts through the heart of every human being. And who is willing to destroy a piece of his own heart?"

Another relevant Biblical inspiration is found in 1 John 4: 17-18. The apostle John wrote there, "In love there can be no fear, for fear is driven out by perfect love."

This idea also resonates with what Alan Paton wrote in his classic novel, Cry, The Beloved Country: "And men were afraid, but their fear could not be cast out, except by love."

THERMODYNAMICS OF GOOD AND EVIL

Maybe you can see where I am going with this. Let's see if we can reinter-pret these classic thermodynamic laws about physical energy to describe the management of spiritual energy, consistent with the inspirations we just heard.

In the citations above, Matthew suggests that our souls are capable of both good and evil, while John suggests that fear (which can lead to evil) can be driven out by God's love. Another way of saying this is that the infusion of God's love is the only way to reduce fear and drive out the evil that we are otherwise capable of. God's love provides the spiritual energy we need to fill our souls with the power to reduce and avoid evil.

The first law of thermodynamics says that physical energy cannot be created or destroyed, it can only change forms. Similarly, God's love is a spiritual energy that can either fill our souls or leave our souls empty. We do not create it or destroy it. The physical energy of the universe is infinite, and so is the spiritual energy of God. It contains infinite possibilities which we can welcome or reject, but it is always there, waiting for us to let it fill our souls. It was created by God before there was time and it cannot ever be reduced or destroyed.

The second law of thermodynamics says that systems not at equilibrium will tend to move toward equilibrium. Equilibrium is a state in which all things are equal and there is no structure. Thus, in the physical world, everything will tend to move toward chaos, unless physical energy is added to maintain the structure of the system. Similarly, spiritual energy, in the form of God's love, may be required to maintain the structure of our souls. In the absence of that spiritual energy, our souls will move toward chaos. In the same way that physical equilibrium is a state in which all things are equal, we can see that spiritual equilibrium is a state in which all things are possible. When that happens, good and evil are equally possible, because there is no spiritual energy present to guide the soul towards what is good.

President George W. Bush famously said in 2001 that he had looked into the eyes of Russian Prime Minister Vladimir Putin and said that, "I was able to get a sense of his soul." But we all know what happened after that, as Putin's policies became increasingly evil. When Vice President Joe Biden met with Putin in 2011, he also looked into his eyes and said, "I don't think you have a soul." Putin looked back, smiled, and said, "We understand one another." So, if Putin refuses to allow God to infuse his soul with love, then indeed, from his perspective, good and evil would be equally possible, and so he could freely choose to do evil.

One important corollary of this concept is that evil can be considered as the absence of God's love. Without this spiritual energy of this love, the soul collapses into evil, in which any course of action is equally possible, since no moral guidance is present. Evil, in this sense, is not a separate force competing with the spiritual energy of good. Rather, evil is a negative state in which there is the absence of God's love to infuse the soul with the spiritual energy it needs to maintain a commitment to what is good. Evil, then, may be like the thermodynamic concept of entropy, which increases as the situation moves toward chaos. In this sense, we do not need to imagine any great demonic or Satanic forces, no "cosmic battles of good and evil." We only need to recognize God's constant and infinite readiness to fill our souls with the energy of divine love. This love, and only this love, is necessary and sufficient to reverse and reduce the spiritual entropy that would otherwise threaten our integrity and lead to our dissolution.

This may be a pretty radical idea. If evil is only the absence of God's love, then there is no need to imagine a separate force, an "evil god" such as Satan (as was commonly thought of in biblical times when people were familiar with the idea of multiple gods). There is only one God (as Muhammad emphasized), a God who is love (as the apostle John described), a God who is infinitely ready to fill our souls with love, if only we will allow it to happen.

The third law of thermodynamics states that complete physical equilibrium exists at absolute zero temperature, which is the coldest possible temperature. So perhaps another corollary is that spiritual equilibrium, the complete absence of any spiritual energy or moral guidance, when chaos, disorder and evil are most prominent, occurs when the soul is the coldest it can be. In this sense, Hell would be a cold place, not a hot place. This is actually consistent with Dante's vision of Hell in the Inferno.

Returning to the Scriptures, perhaps we can say that some people are not intrinsically evil (like the weeds in the parable that will be burned at the final harvest), but rather we can say that they are not good, because they lack the divine infusion of God's love and grace. That is to say, they do not have enough of God's love (which is infinite) to maintain the goodness that is inherently possible in their souls. Furthermore, even the most evil people on earth—people like Vladimir Putin, the Charleston shooter, and the ISIS terrorists--- can still be redeemed, if only they will allow their souls to be filled with the spiritual energy of God's love.

REMAINING OBJECTIONS

Thomas Aquinas famously tried to prove the existence of God, and in doing so he tried to answer any possible objections to his argument. So I will try to address some objections to my argument as well.

First, as we have seen, John wrote (in 1 John 4:16), "God is love, and he who lives in love, lives in God, and God in him." But what if someone does not live in love? What if someone still hates his brother (see 1 John 4: 20-21)? My response to this objection is very simple, that the person just needs to allow God's love to enter into his soul, and once he does that, he will reconcile with his brother and choose to do good.

Second, we have seen that atheists like Vladimir Putin are capable of evil. But not all atheists are evil, even though they may not accept God's love into their souls. Perhaps we can argue (somewhat paternalistically, I admit) that the love is there for them anyway, whether they accept it or not. The second law of spiritual dynamics (as I have reformulated it above) suggests that for them, good and evil are equally possible, so they are free to choose either one. So they can choose to be good, whether or not their choice is based on an acceptance of God's love.

Third, I note that most people who have near-death experiences return to talk about positive experiences of Heaven. But there are a few (20 % according to the research) who return and describe negative experiences, such as going to Hell. So does this mean that Hell really does exist? At this point, I really have no answer, and I do not wish to dispute what people have experienced in these situations. Perhaps, as the third law might suggest, there is a place where good and evil co-exist, and this is what we might call Hell. But I would like to think that God's redeeming grace can help people to avoid going there.

The **fourth** objection is much more challenging. It is the problem of Job, so eloquently restated by Rabbi Harold Kushner in his classic book, "Why Do Bad Things Happen to Good People?" When I was at Notre Dame, I spent a semester of theology studying the book of Job. Perhaps that was an odd thing for a 19 year old boy to think about, but it is still a powerful question to consider. Maybe Father Hesburgh knew that it was something that should be part of a young man's education. The study of Job became even more relevant for me when I became a physician caring for children with neurological disorders. Indeed, why does God allow bad things to happen to good people?

Kushner suggested that God cannot be all good and all powerful at the same time. Kushner observed that an all-good god who is all powerful would not allow bad things to happen to good people, but clearly such things do happen. He concluded that God can be either all good or all powerful, but not both at the same time. Does the argument I have presented here provide a way to resolve this dilemma?

The laws that describe physical energy are self-evident and proven by science. Perhaps we can say that the spiritual laws that describe good and evil are also self-evident and proven by theology. Bad things happen because that, quite simply, is the nature of physical existence. That is the way the world created by God works. The potential for physical things to move toward disorder is inherent in every moment, in every environment, and in every aspect of nature, including every human life. In other words, bad things happen because they can. God did not make them happen. The potential for bad things to happen was inherent when God created the physical world as we know it, as is reflected in the laws of thermodynamics. Bad things happen in the physical world because they can. Since God does not make them happen, we can still believe in a God who is good. God may still allow bad things to happen, since that is the way the world God created works, but God also provides us with the spiritual energy to overcome them.

Does God have the power to make bad things not happen or go away? Stories of miraculous healing suggest that God does indeed have this power, but we humans cannot predict or control it. We can allow God to fill our souls with love, which provides us with the spiritual energy or grace we need to focus on doing good and avoiding evil. This is pretty predictable and reliable. God does have the power to reduce the spiritual emptiness that would otherwise drag us towards a moral equilibrium in which good and evil are equally possible. This is the predictable, reliable and consistent power of God. In this sense, God is powerful because God always provides the spiritual energy that we need in order to be good.

Thus, God is good, because God does not make bad things happen to good people. And God is powerful because God gives us the spiritual energy through faith to restore our souls to that which is good. We may not always be able to reverse the chaos of the physical world, but God always give us whatever we need to reverse the chaos of the spiritual world, which we pray (in the words of Jesus' prayer) will be sufficient to deliver us from evil.

Peace-Making and Spiritual Valorization

A Sermon Given at the First Congregational Church in Natick,
Massachusetts
May 7, 2006

First, I want to say what a great honor it is for me to be here with you today. What I am going to talk about is peacemaking and spiritual valorization, or how to value people spiritually. I will state the "take-home message" here at the beginning so that you can get an idea of where we will be going with this sermon. The key message is that Christian peacemaking happens one relationship at a time, when we realize that all people are equally valuable and loved by God.

Why should we do this? I think the basis for Christian peacemaking can be found in two Gospel teachings: "Love your neighbor as yourself" (Matt 22:39), and "Always treat others as you would like them to treat you" (Matt 7:12). Thus we are peacemakers when we realize that in all human relationships, (1) God loves the other person as much as God loves me; and (2) I must value and protect for the other person what I most value and protect for myself.

What does this mean? Who does God love, and who should I value? My family and friends, of course, and all of us here in this congregation. But also those whom we do not like, and those who do not like us, and those who are different from us for whatever reason. Christ did not make exceptions, so neither should we.

What about people with disabilities? Being with them has been the focus of my work as a child neurologist for the past 30 years. I have learned much from all of my patients with disabilities and their families, including: (1) to see the gifts that they bring to life; (2) to celebrate their presence with us; and (3) to share my joy with them as they share theirs with me. Mostly, what I have learned from them is how to do what I now call "spiritual valorization," or how to recognize the God-given spiritual value in all people, regardless of disability, and how I can try to manifest this in all of my relationships. I have learned that in a spiritual sense, a child with intellectual disability is as valuable as Albert Einstein, and a woman with Down syndrome is as valuable as the Pope.

How can we recognize the spiritual value in all people? Over the years, I came to see that spiritual valorization can be practiced through what I call "the three ways of looking." In every relationship, with these three looks, we can learn to see that all people are equally valuable and loved by God--including, and perhaps especially, people with disabilities.

The <u>First Look</u> is to try to see the world through the other person's eyes, to get a sense of what the other person thinks and feels, to try to understand the other person's point of view and why he or she does things. In a more complicated way, the first look tries to show us how the other person answers the four questions that describe spirituality: (1) Who am I? What is my personal sense of identity? (2) To whom do I belong? Who loves me and who do I love? What are the important relationships in my life? (3) Where do I come from? What is my cultural, racial and ethnic background that shapes my life? (4) What do I value most in life? What is the meaning and purpose of my life here on earth? Basically, with the first look we try to imagine what it feels like to be the other person, what it would be like to be in his or her shoes, what it means to the other person to be alive.

The <u>Second Look</u> is to see the other person as a human being like myself. It is like what the theologian J. S. Dunne calls "passing over" in which we pass over from our own standpoint to another person's standpoint, then return to ourselves with an enriched sense of the humanity that we both experience and share. The second look shows us that we must value and desire for the other person that which we most value and desire for ourselves: (1) life (including health, in the broad sense of physical, emotional, mental, spiritual and social well-being); (2) liberty (including freedom and independence); (3) community presence, inclusion and participation (as in this congregation); and (4) happiness, in the sense of optimism, joy and satisfaction with one's life. The second look completes the cycle of spiritual valorization by sending to the other person the Gospel message described at the beginning of this talk: I love you as much as I love myself, and I will treat you the same way I would treat myself.

But wait, there is more! There is another look to consider. With the first and second looks, we come to realize that, regardless of ability or disability, age, sex, race, culture or sexuality, we are all equally valuable in the eyes of God. When we realize that, we are ready to experience the Third Look, which comes by the grace of God. It comes when we least expect it, like the answer to a prayer. This third look is a glimpse of universal spirituality, a vision of the glory of God, which we can see reflected in the eyes of another person when God allows us to see it. We cannot see the face of God (Exodus 33:20) but perhaps we can see God's splendor with this third look.

Let me describe the experience as I have seen it. 20 years ago I was an expert consultant for the U.S. Department of Justice charged to evaluate the care of persons with epilepsy living in an institution for mental retardation in Oregon (now closed). One of my tasks was to seek out and meet several residents with epilepsy who were living there. We entered a large room that was covered with mats on the floor, on which were lying about 40 or 50 people. All of them had profound disabilities and were unable to walk. Their lives consisted of being taken out of their cribs in the morning and placed on the mat for the day, then being put back in their cribs at night. The staff pointed out the young man I was looking for and I literally had to step over and around all of the others to get to where he was lying. I then bent down, grasped his hand and spoke to him (the same way I would if he were here with us and we were passing the peace of Christ during worship). At that very moment I suddenly had the sense of something universal passing between us and bringing us together in a spiritual sense, and when I looked in his eyes I saw the third look.

The Jesuit theologian Dan Berrigan described his experience of the third look when he sat by the bed and held the hand of a young boy with profound disabilities: "The way this young boy lies in our world, silent and helpless, is the way God lies in our world. To hear what God is saying we must learn to hear what this young boy is saying." Harold Kleinert, a professor of special education, described his experience of the third look when he was a young teacher trying to teach a boy with profound disabilities "the 25 steps of toothbrushing." The boy was resisting his efforts, but then at one point the boy looked deeply into the teacher's eyes and Kleinert saw "a flash of insight into all that life was about, a glimpse into a personhood far deeper and more communicative than all of our measure of intellectual capacity, of human wit and skill." He went on to say, "Perhaps at the very moment we are laid most bare in the eyes of another (even if that other is a person with profound mental retardation), God has his best chance of getting to us."

Thus, I now return to the take-home message that I stated at the beginning: Christian peacemaking happens one relationship at a time, when in all of our interactions with other people (not just in church) we live with and act upon the knowledge that all people are equally valuable and loved by God. For then we see, as Saint Paul said in First Corinthians 12: 4-11, that the Spirit of God lives in all of us regardless of ability or disability. The three ways of looking, as I have described them, may help us to practice Christian peacemaking in our community and in our lives. All of us are needed as members of the community of God, all of us have God-given gifts and skills to contribute to the community, and our community is not complete when we exclude anyone who wants to be present with us. I hope that these few words I have shared today will help us to see this and to live and act as Jesus and Saint Paul taught us.

The Negro Student
A Story Written in 1963 When I Was 16 Years Old

The school was shocked. The teachers discussed it at lunch and between classes; whole social studies periods were devoted to it; students argued it back and forth all day. Committees to see the principal, the councilors, and the superintendent were hurriedly formed and just as quickly disbanded. The school was in an uproar. No one learned anything that day, and no teacher tried to teach. This was much too big an affair during which to try to conduct school. As one student said, "They don't understand! This school is segregated! We'll kill any Negro who tries to enroll!." And if not literally, at least figuratively, they probably would.

Such was the problem. A Negro student was to be admitted to the sacrosanct premises of Arthur Queen High School, by order of the school board, the city, and the state, with Federal sanction and permission. The dangers were obvious, for only two weeks ago the parents of the students had violently agitated against Negroes in the neighborhood. By then, however, it was too late to try to stop the enterprise.

There were a few students, of course, whose opinions were not colored by the childish tantrums of their seniors. There were also the self-imposed guardians of the Negro's rights, hypocrites who would have shrunk away if a Negro had ever approached too close to their persons. But religion does not support hypocrisy, and a few stalwart believers quietly and unnoticeably stuck to the concept of equality under God. Such a person was Vic France.

Vic firmly believed that he should treat all people as equals and equally, although the truth of this was for him, as for others, at best hard-sought.

A seed of prejudice had been planted in his nature, sowed by his parents, which he had at first nurtured, then condemned. This seed he knew existed, but he vilified its very existence. Loath to say aught that might hurt him or his popularity, he yet determined to overcome his self-believed superiority and in every possible instance to show a Negro that he, for one, did not believe himself better than one of another race --- one whose sole difference lay in skin pigment, a mere adaptation to a climate foreign to him. This struggle against his conscience had been difficult, but fortified by the truths and teachings of his religion, he attempted to dissolve it. Vic was sincere. He had not turned in despair to Negroes as a second-rate substitute for white friends, since he himself had enough friends to be satisfied and to be happy. No, his search for equality had been prompted solely by a feeling that somehow the Negro was not being treated right --- that, according to the Bible, his attitude toward Negroes should be the same as that toward his other fellow human beings, the whites. He did not think it fair that one sector of humanity should be treated differently from their equals, so he attempted to correct it, if not in everyone's mind, at least in his own. Hence, when the Negro came to school tomorrow, Vic knew that he would have to decide between that which he knew to be the right thing to do and that which would not lose him all his friends. This was the decision he would have to make, in spite of his previous soul-searching, for many a thing is more difficult in practice than in theory.

Vic said to his friends, "How do you feel about this Negro entering QHS? You know, I think we rather owe it to God and ourselves to treat him as a human. But the idea is still not favorable to me entirely, at least, How about you?"

"Me? I know what I'm going to do," one of his friends said. "I'm going to make sure that darkie will never forget that he was sent here on the whim of some isolated idiot in Washington. And as for the rest of us--- we're all going to make sure that his life here is one big series of catastrophes. It is up to us to be certain that our children won't have to rub shoulders with a bunch of filthy Negroes. I hope you're not going to play the nigger-lover. I wouldn't, if I were you!"

"I don't know, I just don't know," Vic replied.

"Try it then! See what happens to your popularity! See what happens to you!" they answered, and left Vic standing there puzzled. Quickly, he started on his way home, desiring only privacy and a little time to think.

When he got home, his parents also felt they had something to say. Having read the paper, they knew all about it. "Good Heavens, son, you don't mean to say they're going to let a Negro boy in with you children? Heaven forbid! Wait 'til your father hears about this! Now I'm going to tell you something for your own good. You'd better stay away from that darkie if you ever expect to be anyone. Darkies around here are hated as if they were the Devil itself, and I can see why. Why I'd rather have a skunk for a pet than a Negro for a neighbor, for the Negro devaluates property." And so his mother went on and on in her little lecture. When his father came home, he gave it to him a little more viciously, but it was the same prejudice. Fortunately, Vic was blessed with the ability to not always hear what was being said. He acknowledged with occasional grunts and yesses that he was following the harangue, but it made no impression on him. He felt the decision was solely his, and it should not be affected by any preju-diced harangues, even when delivered by his own parents. Accordingly, he went upstairs to privately divine for his own self his true feelings and to decide whether or not he should apply them to the situation at hand.

Well, you've got privacy, you've heard one side of the question, and you know the other side, the one your religion demands, he mused. *What is so hard then? Perhaps it's the sacrifice involved. For I would be sure to lose all my friends if I ever carried out the idea I'm thinking of now. I guess that's the main thing holding me back --- the desire for popularity. But then what good is popularity if it is accompanied by a sense of guilt – of not having done the thing my conscience asked, the thing I really want to do? What good would my 'As' be then? I could never be really secure or trouble-free, if I knew that I had been a partner to a crime such as they plan for tomorrow. I couldn't ever be at peace with myself.*

But I must think of the Negro also. He is not going to have a friend in the world, at least at Queen, that's for sure. And I know that being

*friendless is a tremendously miserable state in which to have to live. I re-
member back in seventh grade when I was shunned and unpopular too ---
how my grades actually went down and my morale plunged. Those were
miserable days, when everyone who went past looked at me with a scornful
look, and the teacher had to assign someone to sit next to me in class. I
remember the times I had to sit alone in the cafeteria, friendless. What a
cheerless, insecure time that was for me! I wouldn't want anyone else to
have to endure that sort of existence, not even if he were my worst enemy,
instead of a Negro I've never met before.*

*What a lot of kids at school are waiting for is someone to take the
initiative and start the friendship. Lots of them, I'm sure, would be ready
and willing if they knew they wouldn't be all alone in it. If someone who
was really popular took this attitude of friendship, there would be many
others who would follow him. But even if someone like me, a person with
only an average popularity, led something like this, I wonder if they would
follow me and treat this visitor like the person he is and not as a repre-
sentative of a race which it is fashionable to ridicule. They, too, would
probably follow the crowd and leave me all alone with the Negro, open
to threats, insults, and abuses, which combined could conceivably put
me back where I was so many years ago, except that now I would have
at least one friend --- if he stayed at school. Then my marks would slip
and I would be miserable again, two things I don't ever want to happen.
Whoever it was who said that friendship is more valuable than gold sure
knew what he was talking about, for that is one state I don't ever want to
lose if I can help it. No matter what the church may say about this, there
is certainly this factor to deal with before the solution can be reached
successfully.*

*But look at the Negro. He probably hasn't ever had any friends in a
white school, and this is going to be a double torture for him. Not only will
he be friendless, but he will be ridiculed and tormented too, which I really
don't think is fair no matter how it may affect me. I can imagine what is
going to happen: he will sit alone in every class, before school and during
lunch; he will walk down the hall and be insulted and baited and taunted*

without end. If he has to go it alone, he won't have any faith in whites of any kind, or any fun at all. The stigma of his presence will be felt in every classroom, and he probably won't learn anything in this school. That is the trouble with enforced integration. While it is necessary, there must be a better, more effective way of achieving the same end. But I must face reality: either I make friends or I don't tomorrow, and if I do one, it destroys my popularity, and if I do the other, it destroys my conscience. What a choice!

Well, if I were to be friends with him I think it's pretty obvious that I would lose everything I prize, including friendship and the grades that go along with this. Friendship is priceless, for no matter who a person is, so long as he is human, he still needs love and affection and admiration from someone besides his relatives. I am blessed in that I know people from whom nothing but good will springs, but all my friends are whites in an all-white school. If I were in a Negro school and were the only white student, why my position would be almost the same as the Negro tomorrow, if they feel like the kids at this school do about those of another race. Undoubtedly, they would think that I thought I was superior to them, and consequently they would make no overtures to become friends. It will be that way at Queen tomorrow, only reversed – everyone will think they are superior to him, and will try to let him know it, no matter what kind of person he may be.

But there is more to it than just this. Their whole race is being mistreated and they deserve to be given a fair shake in all things, whether at the school level, the city level, or the Congressional level. Imagine, in some places they arrest them for resisting. I can't believe our modern society could perpetuate such an outrageous sin of society as this. At the very least, Negroes are entitled to be popular or to have friends. Tomorrow that school is going to see things the like of which it never saw before, and I'm going to be there fighting for the rights of a fellow human. After all, the conscience is truer than the mind, and my conscience tells me to help this one have a good time. I may lose my friends for it, but at least I will gain one new friend, I hope. After all, wasn't one of the phrases that founded our country, "dedicated to the proposition that all men are created equal" and wasn't one of the main elements of the frontier that of every man's equality? How can a simple thing like skin color make such a difference in the way people act to each other? It is nothing short of hypocrisy for people to go to churches, knowing that they have forced the Negroes out of them, for their religion preaches the doctrine of equality. Christ himself was not a member of the society of the day, nor would he be today, yet we revere him as God. The inconsistency of people is abominable in this respect at least. And strictly from a practical viewpoint, don't Negroes pay the same taxes as whites and send their children to school? Therefore, they must be able to expect that their child's education will be the same as that a white is receiving and no worse because one's social class is higher than the other's. How can I be true to myself, my country, and my religion unless I help that Negro have fun tomorrow and ward off the cruel taunts and jibes he is sure to receive? Tomorrow I'm going to be friendly. As for my popularity, I'd rather have one true Negro friend than all the conceited bigots in the world. Next morning, I most certainly will not help or be a partner in the persecution of my fellow human merely because of his skin.

The next day Vic France got up early and went to school a half hour before his regular time. Sure enough, there was the Negro student, sitting alone, with that whole corner of the cafeteria in which he was sitting bare and vacant. He also noticed Tom Roberts, "Mr. Everything" for their class: Student Council Senator, Class President, varsity letterman and team captain in four sports, and one of the nicest all-around boys in the school. He was sitting with the usual boys and girls, but by the look on his face Vic could tell that he would like to be friends with the new student, but was afraid to do so. Vic smiled, realizing the torture Tom was suffering, and determined to resolve it. Slowly he started towards the Negro's table, feeling for a moment like Sidney Carton going to the guillotine.

He was walking almost mechanically now, every moment hoping that his nerve would not fail him. He was conscious that everyone was looking at him, and he saw Tom start to rise involuntarily, then stand up and puzzle for a while. As he approached the table, he saw Tom start towards it also, and was so relieved he smiled again, hoping to quiet the new student's anxiety that he might be part of a plot. Going up to the table and putting his hand on one of the chairs, conscious of everyone's attention, he looked into the fear-filled face of the Negro and saw just another frightened student, like himself before tests, he suddenly thought to himself. Smiling a smile of relief and of a sense of foolishness that he had ever been afraid of this, he asked his fellow student, "Do you mind if I sit here with you?"

This story was written in 1963 when I was in high school. I lived in a very racist city and attended the public high school, which was completely white and also racist. Unlike Vic's parents in the story, however, my own parents worked for racial justice and opposed racism. As their teenage son, I am sure my own ideas expressed in the story in some ways reflected their beliefs. I was aware that courts were ordering the integration of public schools around the country and wondered how I would react if integration came to my high school. My purpose in writing it was simply to work out my own thoughts through the creation of a story. It was not written for a class assignment and was never submitted or shared with anyone at the time, not even with my parents. The language and content of the story reflect the times and also reflect my own immaturity.

When I went to college I became friends with a classmate who was an African-American student from Tennessee. The following poem was written February 22, 1966 when we were both 18 years old. We came from very different backgrounds and tried to understand each other but the gap was too great and we eventually lost contact. I suggested to him once that I should come to visit him during the summer of 1966 in Tennessee, but he said that would not be a good idea. The Klan was killing white freedom riders and their Black friends. I then began to understand what being Black in the south might be like. The poem adds a sense of reality to the ideas expressed in the story above. The message of the poem is simple: fighting racism is a lifelong task for all of us.

ADVICE FROM A BROTHER

Nothing is harder than to fight yourself---
But keep it up, my brother, keep it up:
(I shall, too, I promise.)
Our strong captains are dead and we are adrift:
This river flows unknown and dangerous,
But we can swim, I think.
(Avoid God's tempting security or salvation!)
Your strength might save men from drowning:
And maybe that is life.

Today, Tomorrow and Forever

A Sermon Given at the Thousand Island Park Tabernacle
July 25, 2010

Good morning. This past spring, the pastor of my home church asked me to assist the congregation in considering how we might approach issues related to the end of life. Today I would like to talk about some aspects of these issues.

I suggest that we might approach thinking about the end of life by asking three questions:

1. What do I want to do with the rest of my life? Having reached this point in life (whatever it may be, whether young, middle-aged or old), how do I want to spend whatever remaining time I have on earth?
2. How do I want to prepare for what comes next? How do I want to manage my personal affairs and my relationships with other people before I die?
3. How do I want to make the transition from this life to whatever comes next? Whether I am competent or not, whether death comes slowly or suddenly, whether I am prepared for it or not, how do I want to spend my last hours and days?

Today I will consider only the first of these three questions: what do I want to do with the rest of my life? This is a question that engages each of us at whatever point we are at in life, and it has the immediacy of asking what we want to do today, and tomorrow, and the day after that. This past year, the men's group at my church read a book which I found very helpful in considering this question, and I recommend it to you too. It is <u>Forgetting Ourselves on Purpose: Vocation and the Ethics of Ambition</u> by Brian J. Mahan. Mahan's point is that true happiness comes from discovering and following one's vocation in life, which requires identifying and getting past the social and religious scripts that others expect from us. Only then can we listen to what God really wants us to do. There is much more in the book that is helpful and thought-provoking, and I want to acknowledge its contribution to what I am going to say today.

Some of you will likely remember Pope John XXIII, the old man who was elected Pope in 1958 to serve as a "temporary" or transitional pope until they could find a younger, more vigorous person to serve as pope after Pope John died, which they figured would happen soon. Indeed, he only served as pope for four years, but during that time, he transformed the Catholic Church. Pope John was a humble man who was at peace with himself and had faith in the future. He said many interesting things, but I want to take as my text for this talk today one of his more challenging sayings: **"Every day is a good day to be born, and every day is a good day to die."** I remember when I first read this saying of his many years ago, and it has puzzled me ever since.

Most of us would probably agree with the first half of that statement, but I think most of us would be troubled by the second half. What does it mean to be happy to die today, if that is what is going to happen? Can any of us achieve that state of peace with himself that Pope John had when he made this statement? It has become a cliché to say, "Live each day as if it were your last" (indeed, that was a line in the Sunday comics a few weeks ago), but the real question is, how can we do that?

Let us start by examining the various expectations we have that keep us hoping for something better tomorrow. In the book I mentioned earlier, Mahan talks about the various "scripts" that often control our lives. He tells the story of a young woman who had been accepted to Yale Law

School but chose instead to go into the Peace Corps. At first, his students said, "Oh yeah, that is great, good for her." But as they discussed the case further, the students came to believe, "She must be crazy. No one in their right mind would give up Yale Law School." Society had taught these students that ambition for success is the best thing to pursue, and they could not see how someone could think otherwise.

Actually, there are three types of scripts that control our lives. The first type is the set of social scripts that tell us to pursue worldly success, like going to Yale Law School. But there are also religious scripts that tell us to do good deeds because we will be rewarded in a different way. People who do good deeds often say that they want to make a difference in the world, but they may not ask themselves why. If we volunteer for the Peace Corps or go to help the earthquake victims in Haiti, are we doing this to demonstrate to the world that we are good people? Religious scripts consist of the sometimes subtle messages we get from church that doing good deeds makes us look better in the eyes of God.

Mahan quotes Archbishop Desmond Tutu of South Africa in response to this question, and his statement is literally life-changing. Bishop Tutu said, "There is nothing you can do to make God love you more, and there is nothing you can do to make God love you less." The first part of that statement is the key insight for understanding religious scripts. Doing good deeds on earth is not going to help us obtain extra credits in Heaven. God loves us no matter how many good deeds we do. The reason to do good deeds is to share with others the love of God that we cherish in our hearts. As Jesus said in the Gospel, "Set your hearts on the Kingdom of God and all these other things will be given to you." Thus the most important response to these religious scripts is to find and accept God's love in our hearts and then listen to what God wants us to do.

The third type of script, which Mahan does not mention, may be the most insidious and paralyzing. They are the scripts of everyday life. We tell ourselves that we have so many responsibilities to family, friends or work that we cannot change. Maybe someday later, when we retire, we will have time to think about listening to what God wants us to do. We say, "Right now, I have to pay the mortgage, feed my family, take care of my clients, or give a talk at a conference." These are not really social scripts, because these are expectations we put on ourselves voluntarily. Yet these may be the most powerful influences that keep us from doing what God wants us to do.

There is a way to get past these social, religious and everyday life scripts and expectations. It is really very simple. I realized it when I went to my 40th college reunion at Notre Dame last year. The highlight of the reunion is always the Mass that is celebrated by the president of the University for all of the reunion classes present. Last year, the sermon was given by Father Theodore Hesburgh, who had been president of Notre Dame when I was there. Father Hesburgh was 92, almost blind and walking with a cane, but his sermon was clear, cogent and challenging. He said that he begins every day with the prayer, "Come Holy Spirit, show me the way, show me what to do today." That was my take-home message from the reunion, and it is my take-home message to you today. If we start every day listening to God, then we can end every day secure in the knowledge that we have done everything that God wants us to do.

This is the peace of mind that Pope John had, I believe. It is the peace of mind that David must have had when he wrote Psalm 23. Do not listen to the various scripts that try to tell you what you should do. Seek out and listen to the voice of God in your heart. John the Apostle wrote in his first epistle, "God is love, and anyone who lives in love lives in God, and God lives in him. Love will come to its perfection in us when we can face the day of Judgment without fear, because in this world we have become as God is." God loves us no matter what we do, and all we need to do is to let God's love live in us. Living in God's love will show us the way and tell us what we need to do today. I believe that if we can do this, then we can indeed face the Day of Judgment without fear, comforted by the knowledge that we have done, and are doing, all that God wants us to do.

In conclusion, let me return to what Pope John said. We can believe with him that "Every day is a good day to die" when we know in our hearts that we are doing what God wants us to do, and not necessarily what everyone else expects us to do. But let us take it one step further. Surely, if every day is a good day to die, then every day must be a good day to live. Let us go out today and find joy in all of the small things---a blade of grass, the warmth of the sun, a friend's voice---and find comfort in the knowledge that God will be with us today at the Park, hopefully tomorrow and certainly forever.

86493092R00088

Made in the USA
Lexington, KY
12 April 2018